Daily Walking With God

Daily Walking With God:
90 Short Devotionals to Deepen Your Relationship with Him

Eric Gonia

Dedication

To my beloved wife, my best friend, for always believing in me, encouraging me, and helping me. I love you.

To my children, who have taught me so much through being your dad, I love you.

To all the pastors I have sat under, especially Brother Steve and Brother Jeremy, for teaching me so much through your sermons, providing counseling, and for your prayers.

Introduction

On the following pages, I have simply tried to capture the understanding of God's Word that He gave me. Are there times when my humanness got in the way? I'm sure there are, but I pray not often and say, "Lord forgive me." If there is anything good or helpful in these pages, thank God from whom it was given. There are places where I have shared experiences from the farm and life, but even those experiences were a gift from God. All glory be to God.

If spending time with God is new to you, or you're unsure about this "spending time with God" thing, I want to offer you a couple of thoughts. First, everything in life is difficult at first. Nobody thought we were ignorant when we were babies because we couldn't walk. We realize a baby needs to learn to sit up first. Then they learn to crawl. Next, they stumble. Then they walk, and finally, they run. And there are a lot of bumps and scrapes along the path to learning to walk. It is no different from spending time with God. Don't feel you must sit down and have these profound moments with God from the beginning. Just start. He is the most understanding and loving person you will ever know. He wants to be with you.

Second, if prayer is new to you and you don't know what to say, then just talk to God like you would speak to anyone else. Think about our baby walking analogy from the previous paragraph and just start. You will get better with practice.

My prayer is that you will draw closer to God through this devotional. Father, bless their time with you. Let them feel you near and grow their relationship with you. In Jesus' name, I ask these things. Amen.

Table Of Contents

What If I don't Have a Relationship with God?

Perhaps you are reading this book because you are curious about having a relationship with God, or maybe you have drifted away from Him and want to renew your commitment. May I share a little truth with you?

First, what is truth? The truth is that which corresponds to reality. Let me share the following truths based on the Bible, which hundreds of thousands of Christians have found to correspond with reality.

God created the world perfectly, without sin, pain, or suffering. He also gave humans free will to choose whether to love Him or not. God desires our love and obedience because He knows what brings us joy and wants nothing but our good.

Unfortunately, humans were tempted by the devil and disobeyed God, breaking their intimate relationship with Him and bringing sin and suffering into the world. However, God loves every human and wants to restore the relationship He wants with each person. To do this, He sent His son, Jesus, to die as payment for our sins and rose from the grave to give eternal life to all who follow Him.

To restore your relationship with God, you can accept the payment Jesus made for your sin, believe that Jesus rose from the dead, and choose to live your life in obedience to God. As a result, God will forgive you of your sin, no matter what you have done, and begin to walk with you daily.

Here are some Bible verses to help you understand more:

- John 3:16-18: "For God so loved the world, that he gave his only Son, that whoever believes in him should not perish but have eternal life. For God did not send his Son into the world

1

to condemn the world, but in order that the world might be saved through him. Whoever believes in him is not condemned, but whoever does not believe is condemned already, because he has not believed in the name of the only Son of God."

- Romans 3:23: "for all have sinned and fall short of the glory of God"

- Romans 10:9-10: "because, if you confess with your mouth that Jesus is Lord and believe in your heart that God raised him from the dead, you will be saved. For with the heart one believes and is justified, and with the mouth one confesses and is saved."

If you want to be restored to this personal relationship with God and begin to get to know Him, take a moment to tell Him. Here's an example of what you might say. He's listening.

God, I have sinned against you, but I don't want to live in this sin anymore. I want to live for you now. I know You sent Jesus to die on the cross for my sin and rose Him from the dead. Please forgive me for my sin and help me live for You now. I commit my life to You.

If you just made this commitment to God, I would love for you to let me know by emailing me at eric@ericgonia.com.

God Wants a Personal Relationship with You

In the Garden of Eden, we see God's desire for a personal relationship with His creation. Genesis 3:8 portrays God walking in the garden, with Adam and Eve hearing His familiar footsteps. Though they did not physically see Him, they recognized His presence by the sound. This recognition suggests that such encounters were not uncommon.

Regrettably, this instance occurred after Adam and Eve had sinned, prompting them to hide from God. This hiding echoes the shame we experience when we realize our disobedience to Him. However, God had a plan to restore this precious relationship. While He may not walk with us in physical form as before, He draws near to us through the Holy Spirit. Upon accepting Jesus' sacrifice on the cross, His blood washes away our sins, and we receive the Holy Spirit. Through the indwelling of the Holy Spirit, God's presence becomes intimate and personal. We become His temple.

When we earnestly seek God's closeness, He responds by drawing near to us (James 4:8). Today, will you choose to remain distant from God or draw near to Him? Sadly, many who identify as Christians merely practice religion without truly desiring closeness with God. They resemble Adam and Eve, hiding when they hear God's presence. Instead, let us abandon attempts to justify ourselves through religious acts and seek cleansing through the precious blood of Jesus Christ. Only then can we draw near to God with genuine hearts.

Today's Scripture

And they heard the sound of the Lord God walking in the garden in the cool of the day, and the man and his wife hid themselves from the presence of the Lord God among the trees of the garden. Genesis 3:8

Follow First: Surrendering to Jesus Without Waiting for Perfection

When Jesus called His twelve disciples, He didn't ask them to become perfect before they followed Him. He simply invited them to follow. Jesus has the same expectation of us. Jesus invites us to follow Him, knowing He will gently clean us up as we walk in obedience. Jesus desires your heart and asks you to hear His call and step out in obedience. However, He does want you to be willing to change and turn away from sin, but you don't need to be perfect before answering His call. He has abundant life in store for us if we only surrender to Him and faithfully follow His lead.

Likewise, when Jesus calls you to a task or a purpose, you don't need to be fully equipped before stepping out in obedience. He will equip you along the way. Consider King David. God anointed him, king of Israel, at a young age. He didn't assume the throne until years later. David answered the call, and then God began equipping David as he walked in obedience.

Similarly, when Jesus called His disciples, such as Matthew, the tax collector, He didn't demand perfection or expertise before inviting them to follow. Jesus simply said, "Follow me." He then began transforming their lives. In the same way, Jesus meets us where we are, loves us as we are, and calls us to follow Him.

Won't you stop waiting to follow Him until you are clean and equipped? Simply step out in obedience to His call. He accepts you as you are. Trust in His power and grace, and wholeheartedly pursue Him in obedience.

Today's Scripture

As Jesus passed on from there, he saw a man called Matthew sitting at the tax booth, and he said to him, "Follow me." And he rose and followed him. Matthew 9:9

A Guide to Spending Quality Time with Jesus

Spending time with Jesus is like spending time with any other friend or family member you enjoy talking to. It means finding a quiet place to be alone with Him. Start with prayer. Talk with Him just like you are talking to a friend. Begin this conversation by praising Him for who He is. Next, thank Him for whatever comes to mind that He has done for you or given you. It can be as simple as thanking Him for saving you. Finally, ask for the things that come to mind. The Holy Spirit will bring to mind the things you need to ask for and don't worry about forgetting something. He already knows what you need. This asking is more for your benefit than for Him. You are placing your faith in His ability to answer and provide for your needs.

Notice I said "needs" at the end of the last paragraph. We cannot ask God for frivolous things to satisfy our passions, thinking God will answer them. In James chapter 4, we are told we have not because we ask not. Furthermore, we ask and do not receive because we ask to spend it on our passions. Let us focus on God and others. When we ask for our needs and the needs of others, God will answer in due time. The answer might not be what we expect, as God is a good father who gives us the best, even when we do not realize how good it is.

The above is simply a guideline. The important thing is finding somewhere you can be alone and quiet. Then, talk to Him like you would a friend. However, do not take up the whole time talking. Like talking with a friend, give Him a chance to speak to you. Sit quietly for at least five minutes. Many times your mind will wander. Try to quiet it as much as you can, but do not worry if you struggle to do so. Sometimes we need to let it wander for a while and process everything going on in our life now. Just do not let fear enter this time. When fear of a situation comes up, use that as a prompt to talk to Jesus about that situation. Then, go back to listening.

Finally, read the Word. Jesus will speak to you through the Bible. Sometimes He will make something stand out in the scripture you are reading. However, do not fret if He doesn't. Just like time with a friend often differs, your time with Jesus will differ many times. Remember, He is a real person that you are spending time with. Come to this time seeking Him and His presence.

One other note, if He does not show up one day, ask Him to show you why. It could be there is sin in your life that you need to repent of. When the time is right, and if you seek Him, He will let you know.

Today's Scripture

And after he had taken leave of them, he went up on the mountain to pray. Mark 6:46

Will You Let It Into Your House?

Imagine that I showed up at your doorstep holding a bucket. As soon as you answered the door, I asked, "Can I come in and chat for a while?" You might say, "Sure, what's in the bucket?" And I would reply, "This is the biggest rattlesnake I've ever seen! I caught it behind my house this morning and wanted to show you."

At that moment, you would likely respond in one of two ways:

1. "I don't want to see that thing! Get rid of it!"

2. "Cool, let me see!"

I might say, "Can we go inside? It's hot out here, and I'm afraid the snake will get energy from this heat and move fast when I open this lid."

What would you do? Would you let me bring the snake into your house? What if I had a plastic dish containing a giant black widow spider that I caught in my shop? Or what if I showed up with a petri dish containing the world's deadliest disease, saying, "You've got to see all these colors growing in this dish. It's so cool!"

Why would you not let me in your house? It's because you know these things are dangerous and even deadly. The Bible warns us about how dangerous some things can be. For example:

"Who has woe? Who has sorrow? Who has strife? Who has complaining? Who has wounds without cause? Who has redness of eyes? Those who tarry long over wine; those who go to try mixed wine. Do not look at wine when it is red, when it sparkles in the cup and goes down smoothly. In the end it bites like a serpent and stings like an adder." Proverbs 23:29-33

We might tell ourselves, "Everyone is doing this thing. I'll just dabble in this or that. I'm not going to take it too far." But accidents happen. What if I accidentally knocked over the bucket containing the snake, and it got loose in your house? Would you regret ever letting me bring it in?

The same goes for spiritual matters. What are you allowing into your spiritual home? Are you dabbling in things that the Bible has clearly warned us about? Things go too far even when we don't intend for it to happen. We can end up hurting those around us and ourselves. And when it's our kids or grandkids watching us, they may stumble and take it too far. So be careful what you let into your spiritual house.

Trusting and Waiting

Have you ever waited on someone, unsure if they would show up? We've all been there. Maybe you agreed to meet a friend at a coffee shop, and they haven't arrived yet. As you wait, you wonder if they forgot, got stuck in traffic, or something more serious happened. The longer you wait, the more you begin to question whether they will show up at all.

It takes trust to wait on someone. The time we are willing to wait in a situation like this is often proportional to how much we trust the person we are waiting for. But what about waiting on the Lord? How long are we willing to wait for Him to answer our prayers? Do we doubt Him if He doesn't answer on the first day or even after a week or a month? How much do we trust that He will show up and answer our prayers in His perfect timing?

The truth is that waiting on the Lord can be challenging, especially when we are dealing with difficult circumstances or facing uncertainty. But we are called to wait on Him and trust His faithfulness. As Isaiah 40:31 reminds us, "they who wait for the Lord shall renew their strength; they shall mount up with wings like eagles; they shall run and not be weary; they shall walk and not faint."

When we trust in the Lord and wait patiently for Him, we can have confidence that He will come through for us. We may not always understand His timing or ways, but we can trust in His goodness and love for us. So let us wait on Him with hope and expectation, knowing He is faithful to His promises.

Today's Scripture

but they who wait for the Lord shall renew their strength; they shall mount up with wings like eagles; they shall run and not be weary; they shall walk and not faint. Isaiah 40:31

Protect Your Kids

As parents, we spend a lot of time protecting our kids from the physical dangers of this world. We teach them to "look both ways before crossing the street" and "don't talk to strangers." And rightly so. After all, it is our responsibility as parents.

However, do we spend enough time protecting them from spiritual dangers? Physical dangers may harm them or even take their life, but spiritual dangers will take their soul. Physical death is temporary, but spiritual death is permanent.

I pray that as you spend time with God and read these devotionals, He will reveal important spiritual truths that you can share with your children. By doing so, you can teach them about who God is and the spiritual dangers that exist in this world.

Deuteronomy 6:5-9 says, "You shall love the Lord your God with all your heart and with all your soul and with all your might. And these words that I command you today shall be on your heart. You shall teach them diligently to your children, and shall talk of them when you sit in your house, and when you walk by the way, and when you lie down, and when you rise. You shall bind them as a sign on your hand, and they shall be as frontlets between your eyes. You shall write them on the doorposts of your house and on your gates."

Let us take seriously the call to protect our children physically and especially spiritually and teach them about God and His ways.

Obedience, not Sacrifice

Obedience to God is a crucial aspect of our faith. Often, we may find ourselves caught up in routine religious activities, forgetting the importance of walking with God in obedience and spending time with Him. Through this communion with God, we come to understand His will for our lives. At that point, we have a choice: continue our comfortable routines or obey Him.

God desires our obedience, not our sacrifice. While religious activities such as attending church, tithing, singing in the choir, or teaching Sunday school are good, they should not replace obedience to God. We can get so caught up in these routine religious activities that we miss what God calls us to do. In fact, these religious activities can even take the place of a true relationship with Him.

The prophet Samuel reminds us that obedience is more important than religious sacrifice in 1 Samuel 15:22. Our sacrifice should come as a result of our obedience to God, not as a way to make ourselves feel good.

God does not need us to perform tasks for Him. He also seeks more than our sacrifice to satisfy our need to be "righteous." Instead, He desires that we walk with Him daily and remain obedient to His will and what He is calling us to do. As Micah 6:8 states, He requires us to do justice, love kindness, and walk humbly with Him. Let us strive to obey Him in all things and follow His lead.

Today's Scripture

And Samuel said, Has the Lord as great delight in burnt offerings and sacrifices, as in obeying the voice of the Lord? Behold, to obey is better than sacrifice, and to listen than the fat of rams. 1 Samuel 15:22

Is God Distant?

If you feel like God is distant, it could be because of sin in your life. According to Isaiah 59:1-2, our sins can cause God to hide His face from us and not listen to our prayers.

Recently, I noticed that God wasn't showing up during our time together. It took me a couple of days to realize this because my quiet time with Him had become routine. But when I finally noticed, I asked God why. He told me it was because of my motives when playing the banjo. I was doing it for my glory rather than to glorify Him. I immediately repented and asked for His forgiveness.

If you notice that God isn't showing up in your life, ask Him with a sincere heart and seek Him. He may not answer immediately, but He will let you know why. Remember, our sins can create a separation between us and God.

Today's Scripture

Behold, the Lord's hand is not shortened, that it cannot save, or his ear dull, that it cannot hear; but your iniquities have made a separation between you and your God, and your sins have hidden his face from you so that he does not hear. Isaiah 59:1-2

Describe Your Relationship With God

Who is God to you? Is He just a name you use when you're upset or surprised, or is He a close friend with whom you have daily conversations? Do you see Him as someone always watching and waiting for you to mess up or as a loving Father who wants the best for you?

Has there ever been a person in your life that you thought was one way, but as you get to know them better, you learn they were totally different? I know I have. As we get to know God better through spending time with Him, we learn who He really is. Our perception of God is often clouded by our relationship with our earthly father or by the perception created by the church we attended as a child. To truly know who God is, we must spend time with Him.

In addition, our perception of God can affect our relationship with Him. We may not feel comfortable approaching Him if we see Him as distant or uncaring. We may not feel worthy of His love and grace if we see Him as harsh and judgmental. But if we see Him as the loving, faithful, and merciful God that He is, we can have a deep and meaningful relationship with Him.

So who is God to you? Take some time to reflect on your perception of God and ask Him to reveal Himself to you in a new and personal way. You may be surprised at what you discover.

Today's Scripture

Oh, taste and see that the Lord is good! Blessed is the man who takes refuge in him! Psalm 34:8

Trusting or Anxious?

As I write this devotion, I feel the stress of a busy day and an approaching work deadline. Despite feeling tired, I'm tempted to work late at my job instead of fulfilling my commitment to write this devotion. However, I felt a prompting from the Holy Spirit to honor my commitment, so I followed His leadership.

In times of stress and pressure, our default setting is often to rely on our strength and find solutions on our own. We worry and become anxious, playing out worst-case scenarios in our heads. But as believers, we can change our default setting to instead trust in God.

Philippians 4:6-7 reminds us to bring our requests and concerns to God in prayer, with a heart of thanksgiving. When we surrender our worries and trust in God's provision and guidance, we can experience a peace that surpasses all understanding. We can trust that God is with us, even during difficult circumstances.

Let us pray for God to help us change our default setting to one of trust in Him. May we remember that He is always with us and that His peace can guard our hearts and minds in Christ Jesus.

Today's Scripture

do not be anxious about anything, but in everything by prayer and supplication with thanksgiving let your requests be made known to God. And the peace of God, which surpasses all understanding, will guard your hearts and your minds in Christ Jesus. Philippians 4:6-7

Be Strong and Courageous

In the Bible, we often read the words "be strong and courageous." However, in Psalm 78:9-11, we see the opposite. Armed with bows, the Ephraimites shrink back from the battle and fail to keep God's covenant. They forget His works and wonders and refuse to walk according to His law. It's easy to imagine the fear on their faces and the trembling in their armor as they faced the enemy.

Indeed, the battle for our souls and the souls of others is a frightening reality. We are not wrestling against flesh and blood but against spiritual forces of evil. If we focus on this, we might become fearful and run away like the Ephraimites.

Yet, when we meditate on the faithfulness and power of God to save, we gain strength and courage. We realize that we are not fighting with our strength but with the strength of the Lord. We need armor that is not of this world and a battle companion bigger than our enemies.

As we draw closer to God and get to know Him better, we realize there is nothing to fear. God can handle anything; His faithfulness gives us the strength and courage we need. It's not something we can get from selfish affirmations or self-praise but from spending time with the Creator of the universe. Let us seek Him daily and be not of those who shrink back but of those who stand firm in His promises.

Today's Scripture

But we are not of those who shrink back and are destroyed, but of those who have faith and preserve their souls. Hebrews 10:39

Embracing Change

Life can change unexpectedly and take us in new directions we never thought possible. Recently, the idea of selling our farm came to mind. At first, I wasn't sure if it was God's plan. After prayer and careful consideration, I began to see what God was doing and that putting the farm up for sale was indeed the next step.

As we reflect on the stories of Biblical figures, we see that obedience to God often requires significant life changes. Abram (later known as Abraham) had to leave his family and country to travel to Canaan, the Israelites left Egypt for the promised land, David left his life as a shepherd to become king, and Saul's conversion to Paul completely transformed who he was. While these changes were not always easy, they led to growth, joy, and abundant life for those who chose to obey.

Are you holding back from following God's plan because of fear or a desire for comfort? Remember that obedience to God will likely require change, but it brings blessings and fulfillment beyond measure.

Today's Scripture

Remember not the former things, nor consider the things of old. Behold, I am doing a new thing; now it springs forth, do you not perceive it? I will make a way in the wilderness and rivers in the desert. Isaiah 43:18-19

God's Delight in You

There's a song called "Sweet Beulah Land" by Squire Parsons that touched my heart recently in a special way. Even though I had heard it before, I began crying while listening to it. So I decided to learn the song on the banjo, and while struggling to play it one night, I noticed a Bible verse at the top of my sheet music. It was Isaiah 62:4-5. In these verses, God declares that He delights in His people and rejoices over us like a groom rejoices over a bride. Next, God impressed upon me to look up the meaning of Beulah, which means "married" in the Bible. I WAS ASTOUNDED when I began to put all this together in my head. God actually delights in me as a groom delights in his bride.

Some of you may think that God cannot delight in you because of the things you've done in the past. But if you have given your heart to Jesus, His blood has washed away your sins. God's sacrifice on the cross has made it possible for you to become a child of the King, and He delights in you. He desires to walk with you daily and spend time with you like a newly married couple who can't get enough of each other. God's love never fades, and His grace is sufficient to forgive every sin you repent of.

The version of "Sweet Beulah Land" that touched my heart refers to heaven as Beulah Land. I invite you to scan the QR code below and listen to it on YouTube. Remember that God delights in you and longs to spend time with you as His beloved child.

https://youtu.be/HjwJibYED30 - YouTube link that is embedded in the QR code. If you need to type it in, it is case-sensitive.

Today's Scripture

You shall no more be termed Forsaken, and your land shall no more be termed Desolate, but you shall be called My Delight Is in Her, and your land Married; for the Lord delights in you, and your land shall be married. For as a young man marries a young woman, so shall your sons marry you, and as the bridegroom rejoices over the bride, so shall your God rejoice over you. Isaiah 62:4-5

Five Principles of Prayer

As believers, prayer is an essential part of our relationship with God. However, prayer and how we should approach it is often misunderstood. The Bible provides us with several principles about prayer, which we should keep in mind as we come before God:

1. God already knows what we need. We don't need to come before Him with long, elaborate prayers. Instead, we should come to Him in faith, trusting He knows what we need even before we ask Him. (Matthew 6:7-8)

2. Pray with faith that God will answer. We should approach prayer with the faith that God will answer and move mountains on our behalf. (James 1:5-7, Hebrews 11:1)

3. The Holy Spirit helps us in our weakness when we don't know what to pray. We don't always have the right words to say, but the Holy Spirit intercedes on our behalf, bringing our needs before God. (Romans 8:26)

4. We should come to God in faith, asking for what we need and for the needs of others. We acknowledge that He is the one who provides all that we need. (James 4:2b)

5. We should not ask for things selfishly or for our own passions. Instead, we should ask for things that align with God's will and for the good of others. (James 4:3)

By keeping these principles in mind as we pray, we can deepen our relationship with God and trust Him more fully in every area of our lives.

Today's Scripture

In these days he went out to the mountain to pray, and all night he continued in prayer to God. Luke 6:12

God's Transformative Power

God's ability to change us is truly amazing. As I sit here and reflect on how God has changed me throughout the years, I cannot help but feel grateful for His intervention in my life. I often wonder who I could have become without God in my life. I think about how some of my negative experiences as a child could have left me scarred for life, but God's grace and love have transformed me beyond measure.

As we get to know our Heavenly Father, day after day, He transforms our minds and hearts. He sets a perfect example of what a loving father should be, and as we learn from Him, our beliefs and thinking begin to align with His Word. Spending time with Him and daily seeking to know God better is the best way to become a better person.

When we truly seek to know who God is, just as we would seek to know a close friend or spouse, we open ourselves up to His transformative power. We begin to understand that God is a person, and He wants to be known by us. He wants to transform our lives from the inside out, and when we surrender our hearts to Him, we can experience His life-changing power.

So, let us seek God with all our hearts and minds, knowing that He is faithful and just to transform us into the person He has called us to be. Let us trust Him to change us from the inside out.

Today's Scripture

Do not be conformed to this world, but be transformed by the renewal of your mind, that by testing you may discern what is the will of God, what is good and acceptable and perfect. Romans 12:2

The Importance of Obedience

We had a devotional about obedience a few days ago, but obedience is important enough for another devotional. I once heard a preacher share a story about an older man who asked him what he believed was the most important word in the Bible. The preacher suggested some answers, such as "love" and "faith," but the old man rejected each. Finally, the preacher asked what the older man believed was the most important word, and he replied without hesitation, "Obedience."

At first, the preacher was skeptical, but as he reflected on his Christian journey, he realized that obedience truly is at the core of everything. Love, faith, and obedience are all choices we make, but without obedience, it's impossible to demonstrate love or truly exercise faith. To follow God, we must first choose to be obedient to Him.

Our daily walk with God requires obedience. We must continually ask God to reveal any areas of our lives where we are not being obedient to Him and then commit to reading the Word daily so that He can answer our prayers.

In 1 Samuel 15:22, Samuel asks if the Lord has as much delight in burnt offerings and sacrifices as He does in obeying His voice. He concludes that obeying is better than religious sacrifice.

It's often easier to make sacrifices than to obey God. We may donate money, attend church, or even teach Sunday school while ignoring what God is asking us to do. However, true obedience requires we put aside our desires and follow God's will. While the things mentioned at the beginning of this paragraph are good, why are we doing them? Is it to make ourselves feel righteous before God, or are they done out of obedience to Him? Even when it's difficult, let us choose obedience because "to obey is better than sacrifice."

Today's Scripture

And Samuel said, Has the Lord as great delight in burnt offerings and sacrifices, as in obeying the voice of the Lord? Behold, to obey is better than sacrifice, and to listen than the fat of rams. 1 Samuel 15:22

The Necessity of Rest

Rest is not just a physical necessity but also a spiritual one. When we rest, we allow ourselves to recharge and refocus on what truly matters. In the hustle and bustle of life, it can be easy to forget that we are not meant to carry the weight of the world on our shoulders. God created us to rest and trust in His ability to provide for our needs and guide us.

I'm convinced that much of this world's physical and mental problems are due to people not slowing down long enough to refocus on what truly matters. When we slow down, we gain a fresh perspective and often find solutions to our problems.

In Matthew 11:28-30, Jesus invites us to come to Him and find rest. He promises to take our heavy burdens and give us rest for our souls. When we rest and focus on God, we find peace and rejuvenation, allowing us to continue our work with renewed spirit and energy.

Let's take note of the ebb and flow of the ocean. It comes in, and then it goes out. God designed this same ebb and flow to life. Let us work hard, then rest and trust in God's provision. Let us find rest for our souls in Him, knowing that He is the one who sustains us and gives us the strength we need for each day. God gave us an example of resting on the seventh day. Let us also incorporate rest into our weekly routine.

Today's Scripture

So God blessed the seventh day and made it holy, because on it God rested from all his work that he had done in creation. Genesis 2:3

And he said to them, The Sabbath was made for man, not man for the Sabbath. Mark 2:27

Finding Peace in God

Anxiety can be a common struggle for many of us, often caused by our desire to be in control and know the outcome of a situation. But the truth is, we are not in control of everything. However, we can find peace in God by trusting Him and His plan.

In Philippians 4:6-7, the Bible encourages us to be anxious for nothing and to bring our worries to God in prayer instead.

God promises to give us peace that surpasses all understanding when we give our worries to Him. It's important to remember that this doesn't necessarily mean that our circumstances will change, but rather that we can find peace in the midst of them.

We can also find comfort in knowing that God has a plan for us and that His plans are for our good. (Jeremiah 29:11) When we trust in God's plan for us, we can let go of our anxieties and find peace in knowing that He is in control. So if you're feeling anxious today, I encourage you to pray and trust in God's goodness and faithfulness. He promises to give you the peace you need to face whatever comes your way.

Today's Scripture

do not be anxious about anything, but in everything by prayer and supplication with thanksgiving let your requests be made known to God. And the peace of God, which surpasses all understanding, will guard your hearts and your minds in Christ Jesus. Philippians 4:6-7

And we know that for those who love God all things work together for good, for those who are called according to his purpose. Romans 8:28

Whose Kingdom Are You Building?

Before continuing, I encourage you to open your Bible and read Luke 12:15-21.

In Luke 12:15-21, Jesus warns us of the dangers of covetousness and trusting in riches and possessions. The man in the parable had become rich because his fields produced a bountiful harvest. He thought he had everything he needed for many years and could relax and enjoy his life. He was completely centered on himself and his own pleasures. He was settling into a life of indulgence and would no longer need to seek God or His Kingdom.

However, our life does not consist in having an abundance of things or even having so much money that we think we can now do whatever we want. There is only one place we can put our trust and truly be secure and at peace: trusting God, seeking after Him, and living in obedience to Him. "No one can serve two masters, for either he will hate the one and love the other, or he will be devoted to the one and despise the other. You cannot serve God and money." Matthew 6:24.

It is important to note that having possessions is not the problem, but the condition of our heart toward our possessions is what matters. We should ask ourselves, "Whose kingdom am I building with my possessions and wealth?" Are we building our kingdom of indulgence and materialism, or are we building God's kingdom by using our resources to help others, spread the Gospel, and further God's work in the world?

Let us not be like the rich man in the parable, whose soul was required of him that night. Instead, let us store up treasures in heaven (Matthew 6:20). Let us seek first the kingdom of God and His righteousness, and all our needs will be taken care of (Matthew 6:33).

Today's Scripture

No one can serve two masters, for either he will hate the one and love the other, or he will be devoted to the one and despise the other. You cannot serve God and money. Matthew 6:24

Five Principles of Leadership

Leadership is an important aspect of many roles, including parenting, marriage, work, and teaching. Everyone is leading someone. Even if you are young, there are younger ones looking up to you. You are their leader. There are certain principles you can follow to be a better leader. Here are five biblical leadership principles:

1. Leaders pray for their followers.

    In Exodus 32:8-14, Moses interceded on behalf of the Israelites before God, asking for their forgiveness. Similarly, in John 17:9, Jesus prayed for His disciples, asking God to protect and keep them. Leaders who pray for their followers demonstrate their care and concern for them. God also changes our own heart and mind toward our followers when we pray for them.

2. Leaders lead from a place of serving their followers.

    Jesus modeled this principle by washing His disciples' feet in John 13:3-5 and 13-14. He showed that leadership is not about power or position but serving others. Also, 1 Timothy 4:11-12 emphasizes setting an example and serving others.

3. Leaders lead by example.

    As mentioned in the previous principle, leaders should set an example for their followers. In 1 Timothy 4:11-12, Paul urges Timothy to be an example in speech, conduct, love, faith, and purity. Jesus also demonstrated this principle by washing His disciples' feet.

4. Leaders pray about big decisions and seek the Lord's wisdom.

   In Luke 6:12-13, Jesus spent the night in prayer before choosing His twelve apostles. Similarly, Proverbs 3:5-6 encourages us to trust in the Lord and seek His guidance in all our ways. Leaders who pray and seek God's wisdom before making big decisions show their reliance on God and demonstrate where true wisdom comes from, God.

5. Leaders spend time with God.

   Exodus 34:29 and 34 describe how Moses spent time with God, and his face became radiant as a result. Similarly, leaders who spend time with God will be renewed and strengthened in their leadership roles. Spending time with God through worship, prayer, and Bible reading helps leaders gain perspective, guidance, and wisdom.

In conclusion, these five leadership principles can help make you a better leader. By following these principles, you can lead with integrity, humility, and wisdom and help change the lives of those around you.

Be Mindful of What You Consume

The media we consume has a powerful effect on our thinking. Subtle messages are communicated through television shows, movies, and even music. It's important to be aware of what we're feeding our minds.

For example, consider the impact of Disney movies and shows on our perception of animals. Many of these productions feature talking animals with human-like emotions. This portrayal can lead to a belief that real animals have similar feelings and should not be eaten. Many people that take up this belief have never been around farm animals. Their entire perception is based on fictional movies.

Don't get me wrong. I like a good Disney movie. But I watch the movie while being conscious of what it communicates to me. What are the underlying messages? I'm also not saying the messages are communicated with ill intent, but they are there nonetheless.

We need to consume media thoughtfully and be aware of its messages. Mindlessly consuming media can lead to negative impacts on our thinking and behavior.

As Christians, it's crucial to walk closely with God and listen to the guidance of the Holy Spirit. The Holy Spirit can help us identify and avoid false messages in the media and how they might impact our lives. By being mindful of what we consume and seeking God's wisdom, we can protect our minds and stay grounded in truth.

Today's Scripture

Do not be conformed to this world, but be transformed by the renewal of your mind, that by testing you may discern what is the will of God, what is good and acceptable and perfect. Romans 12:2

The Amazing Things God Does by His Spirit

Looking back at my life, I can see that the most significant and meaningful things that have happened were not the result of my abilities or wisdom but were the result of God moving in people or circumstances to do things beyond my capability. These were free gifts of God that I only needed to claim. Of course, there was work involved and sometimes fear, but in the end, God had a plan that worked for my good and the good of others. The point is this: while we should work hard in our lives, the important things that will last are what God leads us to do and ultimately accomplishes by His Spirit.

The Bible tells us in Ephesians 2:8-10 "For by grace you have been saved through faith. And this is not your own doing; it is the gift of God, not a result of works, so that no one may boast. For we are his workmanship, created in Christ Jesus for good works, which God prepared beforehand, that we should walk in them."

It is important to remember that these good works are not just random acts of kindness or charity but specific tasks that God has prepared for us to do. They are part of His plan and what He is doing in this world. As we trust Him and follow His lead, we can experience the joy and fulfillment of seeing His amazing works accomplished through us. So let us walk closely with God and be ready to do the good works He has prepared for us by His Spirit.

Today's Scripture

For by grace you have been saved through faith. And this is not your own doing; it is the gift of God, not a result of works, so that no one may boast. For we are his workmanship, created in Christ Jesus for good works, which God prepared beforehand, that we should walk in them. Ephesians 2:8-10

Don't Run Ahead

Sometimes, we may think we understand what God is telling us, but we later find out that we made a lot of assumptions about how God will accomplish his will. God may tell us "**what**" He is doing, but He doesn't always reveal the full "**how**." He tells us enough of the "how" to know the next step. Not knowing the full "how" protects us from running ahead of Him and messing things up. The problem comes when we make assumptions about the "how" and run ahead to make the assumed "how" work when God never intended us to get ourselves into the resulting mess.

Thankfully, like a loving father with a child running ahead on the trail ahead of him, He calls us back and pulls us out of the trouble we find ourselves in. Walking beside our Heavenly Father on the trail of life is much sweeter, talking and enjoying His presence along the way, rather than running ahead or lagging behind.

Micah 6:8 reminds us of what the Lord requires of us: to do justice, love kindness, and walk humbly with Him. Walking humbly with God means acknowledging that we don't know everything and need to trust Him for the next step. When we walk in humility and trust, we can avoid running ahead and messing things up.

Isaiah 40:31 reminds us that those who wait for the Lord will renew their strength. Waiting on the Lord means being patient and trusting that God will lead us in the right direction at the right time. When we wait on the Lord, we will mount up with wings like eagles, run, not be weary, and walk and not faint.

Today's Scripture

but they who wait for the Lord shall renew their strength; they shall mount up with wings like eagles; they shall run and not be weary; they shall walk and not faint. Isaiah 40:31

The Love in God's Discipline

In today's society, discipline is often frowned upon and viewed as harsh and unnecessary. However, when done in love and with mercy, discipline can be a powerful tool for growth and development. This applies not only to parenting but also to our relationship with God.

The Bible tells us that God disciplines those He loves. In Hebrews 12:10-11, we read, "For they disciplined us for a short time as it seemed best to them, but he disciplines us for our good, that we may share his holiness. For the moment all discipline seems painful rather than pleasant, but later it yields the peaceful fruit of righteousness to those who have been trained by it."

God's discipline is not intended to harm or punish us, but rather to guide us towards a path of righteousness and holiness. It is an act of love and mercy, just as a parent disciplines their child out of love and a desire for their growth and development.

Furthermore, discipline is a sign of our relationship with God. If we are not disciplined when we do wrong, are we truly a child of His? Just as a loving parent disciplines their child to guide them towards the right path, God disciplines us to guide us towards a life of righteousness and holiness.

God is a wise father, and he knows the right time for discipline and the right time for mercy and patience. As we navigate through life, let us embrace the love in God's discipline and be grateful that He loves us enough to correct us and guide us toward a better path.

Today's Scripture

My son, do not despise the Lord's discipline or be weary of his reproof, for the Lord reproves him whom he loves, as a father the son in whom he delights. Proverbs 3:11-12

Fully Trusting God

We recently began selling our 200-acre farm. While I have verbally put the whole process in God's hands and consciously trust Him, I have not slept well. It seems my mind just keeps running over all the details and scenarios, and this indicates that while I might be consciously trusting God and asking for His will to be done, I have not fully surrendered to His will in this matter.

As they say, talk is cheap. I think part of it concerns the large sum of money we must manage in this transaction. What if I make a mistake? What if I leave too much money on the table? What if someone takes advantage of me? What if I don't get the money I should get for this farm, and someone thinks me foolish or unsuccessful?

In such situations, it's essential to remember that God feeds the sparrows and clothes the grass of the field. How much more are you worth? God has the very hairs of your head numbered. Trusting God means fully surrendering to His will, not just verbally but also in our thoughts and subconscious minds. We must let go of our worries and fears, knowing that God is in control and has a plan for us.

Philippians 4:6-7 reminds us, " do not be anxious about anything, but in everything by prayer and supplication with thanksgiving let your requests be made known to God. And the peace of God, which surpasses all understanding, will guard your hearts and your minds in Christ Jesus."

So, let us surrender our worries and fears to God and trust in His plan. May we find peace and comfort in His presence, knowing He cares for us and will always provide for our needs.

Today's Scripture

Look at the birds of the air: they neither sow nor reap nor gather into barns, and yet your heavenly Father feeds them. Are you not of more value than they? And which of you by being anxious can add a single hour to his span of life? Matthew 6:26-27

The Battle Belongs to the Lord

Sometimes we get so focused on the challenges before us that we forget about our relationship with God. Recently, my daughter got married and moved away. My son is moving even further away. And I am facing a challenging set of interviews for a big opportunity. It feels like there's a mountain in front of me and a huge battle about to occur. But in the midst of it all, God gave me two scriptures that brought me comfort and encouragement.

The first is from 2 Chronicles 20:15, where the Lord tells Jehoshaphat, "Do not be afraid or discouraged because of this vast army. For the battle is not yours, but God's." The second is from Exodus 14:14, where Moses tells the Israelites, "The Lord will fight for you, and you have only to be silent."

These verses remind me that I don't have to fight this battle alone. God is with me, and He will fight for me. I don't have to be afraid or discouraged, because the battle belongs to the Lord. If I trust in Him, He will give me the strength and courage to face whatever challenges come my way.

I don't know what the future holds, or whether I will get the opportunity I'm pursuing. But I know that if I do, it will be because of God's strength and not my own. And even if things don't work out the way I hope, I can still trust that God is in control, and He will work everything together for my good. So I choose to trust in Him and to believe that the battle belongs to the Lord.

Is there a battle in your life that you need to trust God to fight on your behalf?

Today's Scripture

The Lord will fight for you, and you have only to be silent. Exodus 14:14

How Well Are You Sleeping?

With the recent financial changes in my life, I have struggled to get a good night's sleep. It's strange because these changes could potentially benefit me. However, my mind has been preoccupied with the biggest opportunity I've ever had, which required a grueling interview process. Last night, I found myself tossing and turning, replaying the interviews in my head for hours. Ultimately, the decision is out of my control.

But there is someone who is always in control, and that is God. He knows which opportunities are best for us, and he knows what the future holds. If we fully surrender to His will, we can trust Him to guide us in the right direction. Trusting God in every area of our lives can bring peace and help us sleep better. So, how well are you sleeping? It may be an indication of how well you are trusting God.

Today's Scripture

You keep him in perfect peace whose mind is stayed on you, because he trusts in you. Isaiah 26:3

Trusting in God Above All Else

As humans, it's easy for us to trust something or someone besides God. We may find ourselves relying on our savings account, a weapon, a spouse, or a friend to bring us comfort and security. But the truth is, trusting in anything other than God is fleeting and can lead to disappointment.

Trusting in God means surrendering to someone we may not fully understand or see. We may find it difficult to trust someone we can't physically touch or control. However, God is the only one who can truly save us, care for us, guide us, and love us unconditionally. He is all-knowing, all-powerful, and ever-present.

Trusting in God may not always be easy, but it's the only safe place to put our trust. He wants nothing but good for us and has our best interests at heart. So, what or who are you trusting? Let us turn to God and trust in Him above all else.

Today's Scripture

Some trust in chariots and some in horses, but we trust in the name of the Lord our God. Psalm 20:7

The Power of Prayer

God promises in numerous verses throughout the Bible that when we call upon Him, He will answer. Yet, for some reason, we often hesitate to bring our difficulties to Him in prayer. Instead, we try to solve problems on our own, without fully trusting our Heavenly Father to work on our behalf. This approach can lead us to struggle unnecessarily and cause us much pain.

In times of trouble, we need to remember the power of prayer. We can ask the Holy Spirit to remind us to take everything to the Lord in prayer. He will hear our cry for help and answer according to His will. Jesus said in John 15:7, " If you abide in me, and my words abide in you, ask whatever you wish, and it will be done for you."

However, it's important to note that there may be times when our prayers are hindered. In tomorrow's devotion, we will explore what may cause hindrances to our prayers. For now, let us remember to turn to God in prayer and trust in His power to work in our lives.

Today's Scripture

If you abide in me, and my words abide in you, ask whatever you wish, and it will be done for you. John 15:7

Overcoming Hindrances to Prayer

Yesterday's devotion encouraged us to bring everything to the Lord in prayer. However, there are times when our prayers are hindered. Today, we'll look at three hindrances to prayer and how to overcome them.

1. Praying for selfish desires. James 4:3 reminds us that when we ask for things solely for our own benefit or pleasure, without regard for God's will, our prayers will not be answered.

2. Not living with our spouse in an understanding way. In 1 Peter 3:7, husbands are instructed to honor and live with their wives in an understanding way, so that their prayers are not hindered. This applies to wives as well. Showing patience, love, and respect to our spouse is essential for effective prayer.

3. Holding onto sin in our hearts. Psalm 66:18 tells us that if we cling to iniquity, the Lord will not listen to our prayers. We need to confess and repent of our sins, allowing the Holy Spirit to purify our hearts and minds.

Are your prayers being hindered? Take a minute to ask the Holy Spirit to reveal any hindrances in your life and to help you overcome them, so that your prayers may be heard and answered according to God's will. He will reveal anything to you that you need to repent of. If He doesn't reveal anything, then don't worry and move forward in faith that God is hearing and answering your prayers.

How Quickly Our Hearts Turn

It's astonishing how quickly our hearts can turn away from God. In a moment, we can lose our focus on Him and start trusting in something else. Money, wealth, intelligence, or athletic abilities are just some of the many idols that can distract us from God. However, these idols cannot be trusted for our security or salvation.

In Psalm 115:4-11, the psalmist reminds us that those who trust in idols become like them - speechless, blind, deaf, and lifeless. Therefore, we must trust the Lord, the only source of true wisdom, help, and protection. He alone can save and love us unconditionally.

Let us guard our hearts and minds against the alluring idols of this world and focus on worshiping the Lord our God. May we remember that our allegiance belongs to Him alone, who deserves all our praise and adoration.

Today's Scripture

Their idols are silver and gold, the work of human hands. They have mouths, but do not speak; eyes, but do not see. They have ears, but do not hear; noses, but do not smell. They have hands, but do not feel; feet, but do not walk; and they do not make a sound in their throat. Those who make them become like them; so do all who trust in them. O Israel, trust in the Lord! He is their help and their shield. O house of Aaron, trust in the Lord! He is their help and their shield. You who fear the Lord, trust in the Lord! He is their help and their shield. Psalm 115:4-11

Prioritizing What Truly Matters

It's easy to get caught up in pursuing possessions, but they can only provide temporary pleasure. You can only find true joy and fulfillment in a relationship with Jesus. Focusing on acquiring possessions can lead us to stretch ourselves too thin by acquiring too much debt. As a result, we become stressed by the smallest hiccup at work.

While it's important to enjoy the good gifts that God provides, we must not let them become our motivation in life. Money, possessions, and experiences make us poor masters and can distract us from what truly matters. Instead, let us work for the Lord and cultivate a close relationship with Him.

Colossians 3:22-23 reminds us to work for our employers as though we are working for God. However, if our employer is unreasonable and forces us to compromise our values, finding a new job and making a change may be necessary. Let us always prioritize what truly matters and distinguish between good gifts and the best gifts that come from God.

Have you stretched yourself too thin? Is it time to stop focusing on acquiring possessions and enjoy the peace that comes from focusing more on the one from whom all good things come?

Today's Scripture

The thief comes only to steal and kill and destroy. I came that they may have life and have it abundantly. John 10:10

Obedience to God's Will is Key

Many people think that living a Christian life is simply about avoiding bad things and doing good things. They believe that if they attend church regularly, give to the poor, and talk about God with their coworkers, God will bless them. However, the reality is that a blessed life comes from a close, daily walk with Jesus. It comes from seeking Him, His will, and walking in obedience to what He is telling us.

Obedience to God's will is key. It's not just about avoiding sin but also about seeking His guidance in every decision we make. For example, if we are blessed with extra money, it doesn't mean that we should immediately invest in real estate or anything else that seems like a good idea. Instead, we should take it to the Lord in prayer and seek His guidance. He knows what the future holds and what is best for us.

It's important to recognize that just because we can do something doesn't mean we should do it. Our desires and plans may not always align with God's will for our lives. Only when we surrender our will to His will and obey His guidance can we experience the true blessings that come from a close relationship with Him.

In conclusion, let's not fall into the trap of thinking that being a good Christian is just about avoiding sin and doing good deeds. Instead, let's focus on seeking God's will and walking in obedience to Him. Only then can we experience the fullness of His blessings in our lives.

Today's Scripture

If you are willing and obedient, you shall eat the good of the land; Isaiah 1:19

Living for Whom?

When we give our heart and life to Jesus, we no longer live for ourselves but for Him. Are you living for Jesus or yourself? If you are living for yourself, ask yourself why? You cannot provide yourself with lasting joy, peace, or security. Jesus is the only one who can provide those things through a close relationship with Him. So, why live for yourself? We often choose this path due to the enemy's deception, which makes us believe that living for ourselves is the only way to be happy and safe. But he is the father of lies. I encourage you to see past his deception and pursue the life Jesus wants for you - the life that comes through a close relationship with Him and walking in obedience to Him daily.

Don't be deceived into believing that a life of selfish pursuits will bring lasting joy and fulfillment. Only by living for Jesus can we experience true joy and peace that surpasses all understanding. As the apostle Paul writes in Galatians 2:20, "I have been crucified with Christ. It is no longer I who live, but Christ who lives in me. And the life I now live in the flesh I live by faith in the Son of God, who loved me and gave himself for me."

Living for Jesus means surrendering our desires and ambitions and putting His will first. It means seeking His guidance and direction in all things and trusting that He knows what is best for us. It means loving and forgiving others as He loves and forgives us and using our gifts and talents to serve Him and bring glory to His name.

So, let us examine our hearts and ask ourselves, for whom are we living? May we all strive to live for Jesus and experience the true joy and peace that comes from a life surrendered to Him.

Today's Scripture

and he died for all, that those who live might no longer live for themselves but for him who for their sake died and was raised. 2 Corinthians 5:15

Don't Be Hasty

It's easy to get caught up in the moment and make decisions without fully thinking them through or seeking God's guidance. We may think we know what's best for us, but only God knows the plans He has for us. Proverbs 21:5 says, "The plans of the diligent lead surely to abundance, but everyone who is hasty comes only to poverty." When we are hasty, we can make costly mistakes that could have been avoided if we had sought God's will and direction.

This principle applies to financial decisions and all other areas of our lives. When we rush into things without seeking God's guidance, we can end up in situations that do not align with His plan. We must remember to be patient and seek His will before making any decision, no matter how small or big it may seem.

So, let us not be hasty in our decisions but take the time to seek God's guidance and direction. Let us trust in His plans for our lives, knowing that they are good and perfect and that He has our best interests at heart.

Today's Scripture

The plans of the diligent lead surely to abundance, but everyone who is hasty comes only to poverty. Proverbs 21:5

What Is Your Motivation?

Sometimes, our motivation can be rooted in a desire for recognition, praise, or personal gain. Other times, it might stem from a genuine desire to serve and honor God. But even our good intentions can become tainted when we lose sight of our ultimate goal – to bring glory to God.

We must constantly check our hearts and ask ourselves: are we truly doing all things for the glory of God? (1 Corinthians 10:31) If our motivation is anything less than that, we risk losing sight of our true purpose and becoming like the Pharisees. They did good works for the sake of their reputation rather than for God's glory.

So, what is your motivation for the things you do in life? Let us strive to align our motivations with God's will and purpose, seeking to honor Him in all we do. Ultimately, it is not what we accomplish or achieve in this life that truly matters, but how we have lived for Christ and His glory.

Today's Scripture

So, whether you eat or drink, or whatever you do, do all to the glory of God. 1 Corinthians 10:31

Embracing a Relationship with Jesus

As you journey through this collection of devotions, you may notice a recurring theme: the importance of cultivating a relationship with Jesus Christ. Indeed, the essence of the Christian walk lies in fostering a deep, daily connection with Him. Yet, we may sometimes find ourselves burdened by self-imposed requirements or overwhelmed by our own sinfulness. It is crucial to remember that our salvation does not come through works, as clearly stated in Ephesians 2:8-9.

In pursuing this relationship, we must not allow sin to taint or separate us from God. Thankfully, God's boundless love led Him to offer us redemption through the sacrifice of His Son, Jesus Christ. Our sins can be washed away through His blood, and the barriers between us and God are removed. Such is the depth of His love and desire for a relationship with each of us.

Therefore, let us resist the urge to overcomplicate this simple truth and humbly seek God's face instead. Ultimately, it is through His grace that we can experience the fullness of this relationship. May we embrace the simplicity of His love and the joy of walking daily with Him.

As you continue on this journey, remember that seeking Him with genuine humility and surrender leads us into this relationship He desires with us.

Today's Scripture

You have said, Seek my face. My heart says to you, Your face, Lord, do I seek. Psalm 27:8

Becoming a Whetstone

What is a whetstone? Whetstones are used to sharpen knives. A whetstone is made out of rock. I was watching a Youtube video on how whetstones are made. They take large rocks and cut them down into manageable pieces. They then cut the rough edges off the rock so it resembles a rectangle. They then begin to cut the rectangle down into many whetstones.

The Bible tells us in Proverbs 27:17, "Iron sharpens iron, and one man sharpens another." The idea behind this verse is we sharpen each other. However, I have seen people who dulled those around them. Are you a person who dulls those around them or sharpens them?

You can take a rock that has not been cut into a whetstone and try to sharpen a knife. All you will accomplish is dulling the knife. If you take the same rock and cut the rough edges away, turning it into a flat rock, you get a whetstone and can turn knives into razor blades.

Similarly, when we give our life to Jesus, we become rocks that God can turn into whetstones. It's part of the immediate transformation that takes place in our lives. However, we still have a lot of rough edges that need to be cut away. Through seeking God and readying His Word, He begins to cut off these edges and turn us into people who sharpen those around us.

Have you surrendered to the refining blade of our loving Father? Are you encountering Him daily and allowing Him to cut away the rough edges? If not, won't you begin to seek Him today and allow Him to change you into a person who sharpens those around you?

Today's Scripture

Iron sharpens iron, and one man sharpens another. Proverbs 27:17

The Law of Sowing and Reaping

In life, there exist certain laws that profoundly impact our lives, much like how the law of gravity affects us physically. One of these laws is the law of sowing and reaping. This principle is referenced in two well-known passages in the Bible: Galatians 6:7-10 and 2 Corinthians 9:6-10. In both instances, the concept of sowing is presented in different contexts.

In 2 Corinthians 9, the focus is on giving generously to meet the needs of fellow believers in Jerusalem. On the other hand, Galatians emphasizes the importance of sharing our blessings with those who teach us the Word of God. Galatians also addresses the idea of sowing in terms of following our sinful desires or the leading of the Holy Spirit.

In essence, the law of sowing and reaping is summarized as follows: If we sow good things by following the guidance of the Holy Spirit in our lives, we will reap a harvest of blessings. Conversely, if we succumb to the temptations of our stingy, self-serving, and sinful nature, we will reap corruption, negative consequences, and even death. It is crucial to note that the more generously we sow, the more bountiful our harvest will be.

Understanding the law of sowing and reaping allows us to comprehend the profound impact of our actions and choices. It reminds us to cultivate a heart of generosity, obedience, and reliance on the leading of the Holy Spirit. By sowing good things, guided by God's wisdom and love, we position ourselves to reap a rich harvest of blessings in this life and eternity. Let us embrace the power of sowing in alignment with God's will, trusting His faithfulness to bring about a bountiful harvest in due time.

Today's Scripture

Do not be deceived: God is not mocked, for whatever one sows, that will he also reap. For the one who sows to his own flesh will from the flesh reap corruption, but the one who sows to the Spirit will from the Spirit reap eternal life. Galatians 6:7-8

Guarding Against the Pitfalls of Pride

Pride can stealthily find its way into our lives through various avenues. Accomplishments, wealth, possessions, and knowledge are just a few examples that can trigger pride within us. Regrettably, I have experienced the grip of pride in each of these areas, despite lacking valid reasons for such arrogance.

How can we steer clear of the dangers of pride? Here are some practical steps to consider:

1. Stay vigilant and recognize the presence of pride when it begins to seep into your thoughts. Being aware of it allows you to take proactive measures.

2. Remind yourself that any source of pride you possess is ultimately a gift from God, not a result of your own merit. Left to our own devices, we would be incapable. Recognize that God alone grants us the ability, resources, and wisdom needed to accomplish anything, and He can also choose to withdraw those gifts.

3. Give glory to God for His provision and offer Him sincere thanks and praise. Acknowledge His involvement in every aspect of your life and achievements.

Pride is a treacherous pitfall. Throughout my journey, I have witnessed its destructive consequences whenever I failed to keep it in check. Allow me to share a humbling incident from my past. I was once helping a friend cut down trees near his house, and after successfully felling a couple, I began to entertain prideful thoughts about my tree-felling prowess. However, my next attempt ended in disaster when the tree toppled onto power lines, disrupting the entire neighborhood's electricity and damaging a neighbor's fence. I was left feeling thoroughly disgraced. I had to approach the neighbor, explain what had happened, and spend the rest of the day repairing the chain-link fence. Moreover, my friend was charged

$1000 for the resulting power outage. This humbling experience was a poignant lesson on the perils of unchecked pride.

I urge you to invite God to reveal any areas in your life where pride lurks. With His guidance, we can actively guard against the pitfalls of pride and cultivate a spirit of humility and gratitude.

Today's Scripture

When pride comes, then comes disgrace, but with the humble is wisdom. Proverbs 11:2

Surrendering to God's Timing and Guidance

As Mandi and I venture into the realm of real estate investing, I find myself confronted with an old sin: attempting to make things happen on my own. Instead of wholeheartedly trusting in God's guidance and direction, I catch myself rushing ahead on the path of life. I need to refocus on faithfully carrying out what I know to do and prioritizing what truly matters. To help you discern whether you fully trust God, here are some signs to consider:

1. Worry and fear have taken hold of your thoughts and emotions.
2. You neglect important relationships, such as with your spouse or children.
3. Concerns about others' opinions weigh heavily on your mind.
4. Inner turmoil causes restlessness that disrupts your sleep.
5. You find yourself fixated on the timing of events.
6. You are anxious about the unfolding of circumstances.

In times like these, releasing control and allowing God to reveal His plans to you is crucial. Focus on the work He has laid upon your heart and find rest in Him. Remember to prioritize the most important aspects of your life. Trust that God is fully capable and trustworthy. He is in control, and He will guide you through every step of the journey.

Let us surrender to God's timing and follow His lead, knowing that He holds all things in His hands. As we release our grip on self-reliance and embrace a posture of trust and obedience, we will witness God's remarkable ways in our lives. Rest assured, He will bring about the best outcomes when we trust Him.

Today's Scripture

Trust in the Lord with all your heart, and do not lean on your own understanding. In all your ways acknowledge him, and he will make straight your paths. Be not wise in your own eyes; fear the Lord, and turn away from evil. It will be healing to your flesh and refreshment to your bones. Proverbs 3:5-8

Where Is Your Treasure?

Where does your treasure lie? Is it in the possessions of this world or in heaven? According to the Bible, our hearts, what we care about and focus on, are closely tied to where our treasure resides (Matthew 6:21). Treasure represents something of immense value, something we hold dear. While it's okay to appreciate the things of this world, we must not treasure them.

Treasure is something we work hard to attain. But what drives our hard work? Are we toiling for fleeting and earthly treasure, or are we striving for eternal and heavenly treasure?

The treasures of this world fade away, wear out, or are stolen. They never bring the joy or lasting happiness we thought they would. The things of heaven do not fade or wear out, nor can they be stolen. Our joy will be full in heaven, and that joy will never fade.

Let us reflect on our priorities and align our efforts with pursuing heavenly treasures. May our hard work be driven by an eternal perspective, knowing that what we invest in heaven will yield eternal results.

Today's Scripture

Do not lay up for yourselves treasures on earth, where moth and rust destroy and where thieves break in and steal, but lay up for yourselves treasures in heaven, where neither moth nor rust destroys and where thieves do not break in and steal. For where your treasure is, there your heart will be also. Matthew 6:19-21

Safeguarding Your Life: Creating Hedges

Have you established hedges in your life? In the Bible, hedges were walls built around something precious for protection. I have erected a couple of hedges around my marriage to safeguard it. One such measure is avoiding dining alone with other women. Additionally, I try to avoid riding alone with a woman in a vehicle, if possible.

Consider the hedges you need to construct in your own life to protect yourself from sin. Sin is a peril far more lethal than any other threat in this world. Are you actively building walls of protection to keep yourself safe from its clutches? Is there a particular sin that you find yourself vulnerable to? Or do you cherish something in your life deeply and want to shield it from the destructive influence of sin? Seek God's guidance and ask Him to reveal the hedges you need to establish for your protection.

In Matthew 5:30, Jesus uses a powerful analogy, urging us to take drastic measures against sin. While I'm not encouraging you to harm yourself physically, the essence of His message lies in recognizing sin's perils and taking decisive action to guard ourselves against it.

So, let us be vigilant and intentional in constructing hedges in our lives. Let us not underestimate the gravity of sin and the need to protect ourselves from its harmful consequences. By seeking God's wisdom and following His guidance, we can establish the boundaries necessary to preserve our spiritual well-being and the things we hold dear.

Today's Scripture

And if your right hand causes you to sin, cut it off and throw it away. For it is better that you lose one of your members than that your whole body go into hell. Matthew 5:30

Jesus Can Calm The Storm

The account in Matthew 8:23-27 provides a powerful lesson about faith and trust in the midst of life's storms. As Jesus and His disciples crossed the sea in a boat, a fierce storm arose, causing panic and fear among the disciples. Amid the chaos, Jesus peacefully slept, undisturbed by the raging storm.

In their desperation, the disciples woke Jesus, pleading for His intervention. Jesus responded, "Why are you afraid, O you of little faith?" His response reminds us of key truths we can glean from this event.

Firstly, when the storms of life threaten to engulf us, we need not succumb to fear. Even if our circumstances appear overwhelming, we can place our faith in God. He is with us, and He protects us through every storm.

Secondly, instead of waiting until our situations reach a breaking point, we can turn to Jesus, seeking His intervention and peace during our storms. By seeking Him earlier, we can experience His calming presence and supernatural power in the face of adversity.

Lastly, the story underscores Jesus' unlimited authority and ability to handle any storm. No matter how daunting or impossible our challenges may seem, Jesus remains capable of bringing calmness and order to the chaos we face.

Let us approach life's storms with unwavering trust in Jesus, knowing He is always with us, ready to navigate us through our challenges. Rather than allowing fear to consume us, let us anchor ourselves to the unshakable one who can calm the storm.

Today's Scripture

And behold, there arose a great storm on the sea, so that the boat was being swamped by the waves; but he was asleep. And they went and woke him, saying, Save us, Lord; we are perishing. And he said to them, Why are you afraid, O you of little faith? Then he rose and rebuked the winds and the sea, and there was a great calm. Mathew 8:24-26

Who's Will Are You Seeking?

I have noticed many Christians lose sight of following God's will by becoming engrossed in doing good deeds. I've even found myself there. We become engaged in activities that boost our self-righteousness. For example, my son Garrett is preparing to relocate to Florida for a new job in a few weeks. Until then, he has been visiting us on Sunday afternoons. While I strongly desire to support our church plant in Charlotte by actively participating and contributing, doing so would mean sacrificing my remaining precious moments with my son. God has unmistakably shown me that He wants me to prioritize spending these few weeks with Garrett as much as possible.

In this situation, if I were to prioritize my desires instead of following God's will, I might attend church and support the new church plant. However, by doing so, I would be driven by my own will rather than submitting to the will of God. We must recognize whether we are truly aligning ourselves with God's will or merely pursuing activities that seem good in our own eyes.

Following our own will does not necessarily entail engaging in malicious deeds. In fact, we may find ourselves involved in numerous commendable actions. However, the pivotal question remains: Are these good deeds what God truly desires for us?

So, I ask you: Are you faithfully pursuing God's will or primarily focused on your desires? It is essential to discern whether our good deeds align with God's plan for us. Let us constantly seek His guidance, surrendering our will and desires to follow His path faithfully.

Today's Scripture

Therefore do not be foolish, but understand what the will of the Lord is. Ephesians 5:17

Embracing Obedience and Trust

We need not become consumed with whether we succeed or fail. It is easy to fear failure, as we don't want to be labeled a failure. Ironically, this fear can sometimes hinder our progress and cause us to stumble. We become so fixated on this fear that we lose sight of the task that God has entrusted to us.

In my current career, I face unprecedented challenges as I embark on a new job. I often worry that I won't be able to meet the expectations of my job and achieve the level of success I desire. However, the truth is that success or failure ultimately rests in God's hands. My sole responsibility is to obey Him and trust He knows what is best for me.

When we obey and trust in God, we free ourselves from the burden of seeking worldly success. Instead, we can focus on faithfully carrying out God's will. The outcome, whether it be success or failure in the eyes of the world, is ultimately in God's control. We must trust Him completely and surrender our anxieties and fears to His loving guidance.

By embracing obedience and trust, we can find peace knowing that God's plan for our lives will unfold as it should. Let go of the fear of failure, for God's wisdom surpasses our limited understanding. Rest assured that when we faithfully follow His lead, we are on the path to true fulfillment, regardless of the worldly outcome.

Today's Scripture

Have I not commanded you? Be strong and courageous. Do not be frightened, and do not be dismayed, for the Lord your God is with you wherever you go. Joshua 1:9

God's Timing Is Perfect

A few years ago, I conversed with my neighbor across the street regarding the potential sale of his house. He said he would speak with his wife and get back to me.

My wife and I had been living in an RV after previously traveling the country with our kids. We were ready to upgrade to a larger home. However, when I didn't receive a response from my neighbor about selling his house, Mandi and I decided to embark on the journey of building our own home.

We obtained estimates, had plans drawn, and navigated the financial aspects, including pre-appraisal for the loan. Unfortunately, during this time, building material prices skyrocketed, and the house's appraised value wouldn't cover the anticipated construction costs. To move forward, we would need to bring additional funds to the table for financing.

During this uncertain situation, we turned to prayer, seeking God's guidance on whether to proceed or pursue another property. During my quiet time with God one morning, the Holy Spirit impressed upon me: "It sure would be nice if my neighbor would text and ask if I'm still interested in purchasing his house." Remarkably, around 9 a.m. that same morning, I received a text from my neighbor with nearly those exact words. We recognized this as guidance from God and chose to move forward with purchasing his house, despite the significant repairs it required.

Looking back, we can now see that it was God's plan all along. Shortly after purchasing, real estate prices began to rise sharply. We sold the entire farm and house for a substantial profit a year later. Although we hadn't anticipated such an outcome when we initially purchased, we now understand God's timing and plan were perfect.

God's timing is flawless in every circumstance. When we trust Him and obediently follow His guidance, we can be confident that we are on the right path, even when it may seem contrary to our understanding. It's crucial to ensure that we are aligned with God's will rather than solely following our desires or the opinions of others.

So, let us have confidence that God's plan unfolds according to His perfect timing, and we can rest assured that obedience to His will never leads us astray.

Today's Scripture

My times are in your hand; rescue me from the hand of my enemies and from my persecutors! Psalm 31:15

Discovering God's Will

How can we discern God's will? How can I know what He wants me to do or make the right decision in a given situation? These are common questions when it comes to understanding God's will. The good news is that the answer is simple. First and foremost, let's address one important aspect: God will never lead you to do something that contradicts His Word. You don't need to question whether lying is His will. His Word clearly states that lying is wrong. So, that's the straightforward part. However, it is essential to familiarize yourself with what the Bible says by investing time in reading and studying it.

The second aspect of knowing God's will involves walking with Him daily. Consider this: What better way to understand someone's desires than walking and talking with them daily? Dedicate time to seeking a deeper understanding of who God is without any ulterior motives or personal agendas.

Furthermore, don't hesitate to ask God. Bring your decisions before Him and request His guidance in revealing the right path. Finally, seek counsel from mature believers in your life. He often employs our relationship with Him and the wisdom of fellow believers to illuminate His plans for us.

By combining your personal relationship with God, reading His Word, and the wisdom of fellow believers, you can uncover and navigate God's will. Remember, seeking God's will is an ongoing process that requires continuous communication with Him and a heart open to His leading.

Today's Scripture

For you have need of endurance, so that when you have done the will of God you may receive what is promised. Hebrews 10:36

Discovering God's Will Part 2

In today's devotion, let's delve deeper into seeking God's will. Imagine you are faced with a decision or in need of God's guidance in a particular situation. Start by getting alone with God and talking with Him about whatever it is.

In this moment of seeking God's direction, we must release our desires for a particular answer to prevent our will from obstructing our ability to see His will. We must genuinely seek to align our desires with what God wants.

Now comes the moment of truth. Do you genuinely believe God's answer is what's best for you or the person you're praying for? There is no doubt God has our best interests in mind. You can trust whatever answer He gives is the absolute best for you and those around you.

Lastly, as you seek God's help in making decisions or seeking His guidance in a situation, firmly believe He WILL answer. This confidence is an active demonstration of our faith. When we come to God with our requests, we do so with the unwavering belief that not only does He possess the answers, but He will also provide them in due time.

Today's Scripture

And he withdrew from them about a stone's throw, and knelt down and prayed, saying, Father, if you are willing, remove this cup from me. Nevertheless, not my will, but yours, be done. Luke 22:41-42

Finding True Hope in God

God is indeed a God of hope, and His Word reminds us of the profound connection between trust and the abundance of joy, peace, and hope that flow from Him. Today's verse emphasizes that as we trust God, He fills us with joy and peace that surpasses understanding. Through this act of believing and relying on Him, we experience the indwelling of the Holy Spirit, who becomes a source of hope within us.

When we choose not to trust in God and instead place our trust in ourselves or others, we miss out on the fullness of joy, peace, and hope that only He can provide. Human efforts may fall short, but God's faithfulness and goodness never waver.

As we navigate life's challenges and uncertainties, let us consciously choose to trust in the Lord our God. Let us anchor ourselves in His promises, seeking His guidance and leaning on His strength. In doing so, we experience abundant joy, peace, and hope that flow from a deep and unwavering trust in our loving and faithful God.

Today's Scripture

May the God of hope fill you with all joy and peace in believing, so that by the power of the Holy Spirit you may abound in hope. Romans 15:13

Where Does Your Help Come From?

In our current deliberations over real estate investing, Mandi and I face a challenging decision. We are nearing the end of an 18-year property cycle. The uncertainty surrounding the market raises questions about whether it is wise to proceed. We acknowledge the possibility of a significant real estate correction on the horizon.

However, we also recognize the potential for substantial cash flow that could arise from investing at this time. It's a challenging decision as we weigh the risks and rewards. Yet, ultimately, we find solace in knowing that only the Lord possesses a complete understanding of the future and what lies ahead.

Placing our trust in Him, we surrender our concerns and uncertainties, confident that He will provide the guidance we need. We find comfort in knowing we rely on God's wisdom and discernment, which gives us a sense of security, knowing that the Lord will lead us along the right path.

Is there something in your life you need to surrender to God? Don't look to others or yourself for help. Look to the one true God who can guide, protect, and be our ever-present help.

Today's Scripture

I lift up my eyes to the hills. From where does my help come? My help comes from the Lord, who made heaven and earth. He will not let your foot be moved; he who keeps you will not slumber. Psalm 121:1-3

The Fear of Loss

For much of my life, I have been plagued by the fear that God may withdraw His blessings. The story of Job has left a mark on my heart. I constantly worry that my sins might lead God to revoke His favor. To alleviate this fear, I frequently seek forgiveness, ensuring that no sin lingers in my life or the lives of my loved ones.

There is no doubt God bestows good things upon us. Yet, sometimes, He allows these blessings to be temporarily taken away to fulfill His greater purpose. In these moments, we must remember His ultimate plan, which is for the good of all who make Him the Lord of their lives.

Sometimes, God permits circumstances that may not initially appear good. Sometimes these trials are meant to deepen our relationship with Him. Sometimes the purpose may involve the salvation of someone close to us. We must ask ourselves whether we are fully surrendered to His purpose or merely pursuing our ambitions. Are we willing to be a living sacrifice for Him, or do we seek personal gain?

It is essential to recognize that only God's purpose can bring us enduring joy and fulfillment, even if we must endure seasons of pain and sorrow. True and lasting joy is found in aligning our lives with His divine plan, trusting that His wisdom and love surpass our limited understanding.

Let us release our fears and anxieties, embracing God's purpose for our lives. In doing so, we discover a profound sense of peace, knowing that our lives are directed by the One who holds all things in His hands. May we find solace in the truth that God's purpose transcends our present circumstances.

Today's Scripture

Oh, the depth of the riches and wisdom and knowledge of God! How unsearchable are his judgments and how inscrutable his ways! For who has known the mind of the Lord, or who has been his counselor? Or who has given a gift to him that he might be repaid? For from him and through him and to him are all things. To him be glory forever. Amen. I appeal to you therefore, brothers, by the mercies of God, to present your bodies as a living sacrifice, holy and acceptable to God, which is your spiritual worship. Romans 11:33-12:1

Love Your Neighbor

Jesus instructed us to love our neighbor as ourselves, ranking it as the second greatest commandment. It's important to reflect on how well we live out this commandment in our daily interactions, whether with our spouse, parents, siblings, or others.

During our walks together on my lunch breaks, I recently realized a pattern in my conversations with my wife, Mandi. I often dominate the discussions, focusing on topics that interest me without actively inquiring about her thoughts and feelings. This realization has prompted me to make a change.

Starting today, I encourage you to embrace the art of listening to those closest to you and truly understanding what is on their hearts. By approaching conversations with genuine interest and curiosity, we can allow them to express themselves openly. This interest will not only demonstrate love as Christ commanded; it allows us to cultivate deeper connections with our loved ones.

Let us embark on this journey of intentional listening. Let's value and cherish the thoughts and emotions of those around us. As we prioritize understanding and empathizing with others, we will love our neighbors as ourselves and foster stronger relationships in the process.

Today's Scripture

And he said to him, You shall love the Lord your God with all your heart and with all your soul and with all your mind. This is the great and first commandment. And a second is like it: You shall love your neighbor as yourself. Matthew 22:37-39

Seeking Godly Counsel

The guidance of wise counsel is a gift from God that directs our paths. If you lack godly advisors, I encourage you to seek them out.

As mentioned in a previous devotional, Mandi and I are considering a real estate investment. In addition to prayer, we have diligently sought counsel from other mature believers. As a result, a clear path has emerged. Without the counsel of mature believers and godly advisors, we would still be scratching our heads about what to do.

So where do you find godly advisors? Assuming you are gathering with other believers regularly, look around that gathering and see who the mature believers are. Now don't mistake age for being spiritually mature. You must get to know people before you can discern their maturity in Christ.

Once you find them, build a relationship with them, not seeking anything in return. As a result, when the need arises, you will have godly counselors in your life.

Today's Scripture

Without counsel plans fail, but with many advisers they succeed.
Proverbs 15:22

All Good Things Come From The Lord

In our walk with God, we must recognize that all good things come from Him. It's great to express gratitude and praise for the blessings He has bestowed upon us. However, I want you to think about how knowing that all good things come from the Lord is also an attitude of trust.

When we don't trust God, we are tempted to try and create or attain good things through our efforts. The truth is every good thing comes from God ultimately. They come through His grace and provision.

By acknowledging that all good things come from God, we shift our focus from our strength and abilities to relying on His unfailing love and faithfulness. We can trust in His guidance, provision, and perfect timing. Rather than placing our trust in earthly possessions, achievements, or human solutions, we anchor our faith firmly in the source of all good things.

May the truth that all good things come from the Lord sink deep into our minds and hearts. Leading us to an attitude of trust in Him.

Today's Scripture

Every good gift and every perfect gift is from above, coming down from the Father of lights with whom there is no variation or shadow due to change. James 1:17

Depart From Me, I Never Knew You

Not everyone who says to me, Lord, Lord, will enter the kingdom of heaven, but the one who does the will of my Father who is in heaven. On that day many will say to me, Lord, Lord, did we not prophesy in your name, and cast out demons in your name, and do many mighty works in your name? And then will I declare to them, I never knew you; depart from me, you workers of lawlessness. Matthew 7:21-23

In Matthew 7:21-23, it is astounding to see how those whom Jesus addresses had performed remarkable acts in His name. They prophesied, cast out demons, and accomplished mighty works. Yet, these deeds fell short. The crucial phrase here is "I never knew you." True Christianity is not merely about engaging in good deeds such as attending church, reading the Bible, or giving tithes. One could diligently do all these and still hear Jesus say, "Depart from me, I never knew you."

Now stick with me for a minute. Consider the significance of Hebrews 11:6: "Without faith, it is impossible to please Him, for whoever would draw near to God must believe that He exists and that He rewards those who seek Him." A key word in this verse is "seek." Pleasing God necessitates actively seeking Him.

Think back to when you were courting your spouse. You earnestly sought to know them, spend time with them, and demonstrate your love for them through your actions. You relished hearing their voice and discovering more about them. Seeking God is like this. We must seek to spend time with him, demonstrate our love for Him, and discover more about Him.

Dear friends, our Christianity must transcend mere religion. It must be a genuine relationship with the Creator of the universe. Let us diligently seek to know Jesus with our whole hearts.

The Things of the World

1 John warns us about the things that are not from the Father and advises against loving the world and its attractions (1 John 2:15-16). Take a moment to read Today's Scripture, and then let us explore the three aspects mentioned:

1. Desires of the flesh: This encompasses not only sexual immorality but also our inclination toward rebellion, which can lead to various forms of sin. We must recognize and resist these temptations, seeking instead to align our desires with God's will.

2. Desires of the eyes: This refers to the covetousness that arises when we yearn for things we see but do not possess. It is a reminder that true contentment is found in godliness rather than in accumulating worldly possessions (1 Timothy 6:6).

3. Pride of life: This pertains to the arrogance accompanying our possessions and accomplishments. It reminds us that our worth and significance come from our relationship with God, not from the material possessions we acquire or the status we attain.

As His followers, Christ calls us to set our hearts and affections on things above rather than being trapped by the world's allurements. By embracing humility, contentment, and obedience to God's Word, we can overcome the desires of the flesh, the desires of the eyes, and the pride of life.

Are you being led astray by one or more of the things of this world? I encourage you to take a moment to ask God to deliver you from whatever might be keeping you from knowing the fullness of God's love, joy, and peace.

Today's Scripture

Do not love the world or the things in the world. If anyone loves the world, the love of the Father is not in him. For all that is in the world—the desires of the flesh and the desires of the eyes and pride in possessions—is not from the Father but is from the world. 1 John 2:15-16

Walking with God: Trusting His Timing

It is common to feel eager for the next big thing to happen, especially when we believe God is leading us in a particular direction. However, we must remember that God's timing is always perfect. When He reveals His plans for us, we must resist the temptation to rush ahead without His guidance.

Often, we become so focused on the "what" of God's plan that we neglect the importance of walking with Him through the "how." We can easily find ourselves in trouble when we run ahead without His presence and leading. Yet, when we patiently wait on Him, we experience the wisdom and protection that come from aligning ourselves with His perfect timing.

Are you tempted to rush ahead of God's leading in any area of your life? It could be a personal ambition, a decision you are eager to make, or a desire for the next step in your journey. Instead of rushing ahead, commit to actively waiting on God. Seek His guidance through prayer, and be open to taking the steps He reveals to you in the present moment.

Waiting on God does not mean being passive. It means actively seeking His leadership and taking the necessary steps aligned with His will. Sometimes, God uses waiting periods to refine and prepare us for what lies ahead. Embrace this time of waiting by investing in learning and cultivating a closer relationship with Him.

We were on vacation in the Smokey Mountains some time ago. There are a lot of black bears in the Smokey Mountains. As we were hiking one of the trails, we came upon a gentleman and his family watching a black bear just off the trail. He told us a few moments earlier he rounded the bend in the trail, and the black bear was in front of him, staring him in the eyes. Thankfully, the bear decided to exit the trail rather than attack.

Our children often run ahead of us on the hiking trail. I thought about what could have happened if they had run up around the bend and encountered this bear. Similarly, we often run ahead of God on the trail of life. Straying too far ahead or lagging behind can lead to trouble, but when we maintain a close relationship with Him and walk with Him, we find guidance, protection, and joy.

So, let us actively wait on God, trusting His timing and cherishing the relationship that develops as we walk together. Seek His guidance in each step, and we will find peace, wisdom, and joy as we journey hand in hand with our Heavenly Father.

Today's Scripture

Wait for the Lord; be strong, and let your heart take courage; wait for the Lord! Psalm 27:14

The Deceptive Tactics of Satan

In a recent dream, I experienced a scenario where my loved ones and I visited the home of a seemingly good man we didn't know well. However, our visit turned into a dangerous trap orchestrated by this man. While my pastor, Brother Steve, and I escaped, my wife and two other family members remained trapped. Our attempts to free them alone or seek help from the authorities proved futile due to the cunning nature of the man.

Upon seeking God's interpretation of the dream, I realized that the man symbolized Satan. His tactics mirror how he operates in our lives. Initially, he lures us with something that appears enjoyable or fulfilling, even if it may not be an outright sin. Through these enticing experiences, he gains a foothold in our lives. Once he has us hooked, he gradually leads us deeper into sin, attempting to trap both us and our loved ones. Though some of us may escape his clutches, the consequences of his traps can devastate the lives of those we hold dear.

Faith is crucial to combat Satan's schemes. We have a choice: either we believe that God's ways and obedience to Him lead to genuine joy, or we listen to the deceptive whispers of Satan, who convinces us that we will miss out on something good. He tempts us to believe we can indulge in certain behaviors as long as we don't cross a line.

We must recognize that these are all lies. While we may escape the immediate consequences as Satan begins to close the trap, our loved ones might not be as fortunate. True joy and fulfillment lie in obedience to God alone, for He is the only one who speaks the truth.

Satan seeks our destruction, and we must remain vigilant. We must remember that everything he says is a lie. If we choose to listen to him, he will deceive us and trap us and those we love.

To navigate this life, we must rely on our personal relationship with Jesus Christ. He serves as our guide, helping us avoid the traps and pitfalls the enemy sets. By obeying His Word, embracing His truth, and seeking His wisdom, we can discern Satan's tactics and walk in the path of righteousness.

Is there an area in your life where you are listening to Satan's lies? Ask God to reveal it to you, and then seek His guidance in escaping before it is too late.

Today's Scripture

Be sober-minded; be watchful. Your adversary the devil prowls around like a roaring lion, seeking someone to devour. 1 Peter 5:8

Embracing Abundant Life Through Surrender

In Matthew 16:25, Jesus imparts profound wisdom about the nature of our lives. Take a moment to read it in the Today's Scripture section.

At this present time in the United States, losing our life does not necessarily mean death. Recently, my pastor shared valuable insights on this verse. We must first define what constitutes our life to understand the message Jesus is delivering. Our life encompasses our possessions, worldly attachments, careers, families, and even the opinions of others. It encompasses everything that forms our existence in this world.

We face a crucial choice: to cling tightly to these earthly things or to surrender them obediently to God. Those who fiercely hold on to their worldly life will ultimately lose out on eternal life and the abundant life God desires for us to experience. However, those who willingly submit to God's direction for them will gain eternal life and the abundant life He intends for us.

Choosing to preserve our earthly life may only grant us a mere fraction, a meager 10%, of the life we could have truly lived. On the other hand, relinquishing control and embracing wholehearted obedience to God enables us to taste the fullness of the abundant life He has prepared for us, the entire 100%. It requires us to release our fears, trusting that God's plans for us far surpass anything we could imagine.

Are you willing to relinquish the reins and wholeheartedly obey God's call? Surrender to His will. You will be astounded by the extraordinary life God bestows upon those willing to release their grip on their life in this world.

Today's Scripture

Then Jesus told his disciples, If anyone would come after me, let him deny himself and take up his cross and follow me. For whoever would save his life will lose it, but whoever loses his life for my sake will find it. Matthew 16:24-25

But seek first the kingdom of God and his righteousness, and all these things will be added to you. Matthew 6:33

The Seeds We Sow: Choosing Our Investments Wisely

In life's journey, making wise choices regarding our investments is essential. Just as putting all our money into depreciating assets like cars, TVs, and house trailers leads to financial setbacks, sowing our energy and resources into temporary and worldly pursuits leaves us unfulfilled.

The principle of wise investment extends beyond material possessions. When we constantly seek to satisfy our fleshly desires, we discover that their pleasure is fleeting and unsatisfying. The enemy deceives us, leading us to believe that indulging in earthly pleasures will bring lasting happiness. However, the truth is that such pursuits only leave us wanting more, trapped in an endless cycle of discontentment.

To experience true abundance in joy, happiness, faith, love, and peace, we must redirect our focus and sow seeds led by the Spirit. By seeking a deep and intimate relationship with the one true God and walking in obedience to His commands, we open ourselves to a fulfilling life. We find abundant life by aligning ourselves with His purposes and surrendering our selfish ambitions.

What seeds are you sowing? Rather than chasing temporary pleasures, let us prioritize a life devoted to seeking God's guidance and obeying His Word. In doing so, we discover a life of true significance and enduring fulfillment rooted in the love, joy, and peace only He can provide.

Today's Scripture

Now the works of the flesh are evident: sexual immorality, impurity, sensuality, idolatry, sorcery, enmity, strife, jealousy, fits of anger, rivalries, dissensions, divisions, envy, drunkenness, orgies, and things like these. I warn you, as I warned you before, that those who do such things will not inherit the kingdom of God. But the fruit of the Spirit is love, joy, peace, patience, kindness, goodness, faithfulness, gentleness, self-control; against such things there is no law. Galatians 5:19-23

What Fruit Is Your Life Generating?

We humans often fixate on external appearances. Did we attend church? Abstain from drunkenness or immorality? Read the Bible? Bring devotions or even sermons at church? These are outward actions that even nonbelievers can carry out.

1 Samuel 16:7 tells us, "For the Lord sees not as man sees: man looks on the outward appearance, but the Lord looks on the heart." What will God find when He looks at your heart? Will He find more than a person striving to perform good works like attending church, reading the Bible, and giving tithes? While these are commendable actions, they do not make us righteous before God.

The Pharisees of Jesus' time did the same, and He rebuked them, stating they belonged to their father, the devil. Our Christianity must transcend mere religion. Attending church, reading the Bible, and giving tithes are only religious acts if the sole purpose is to appear righteous.

Consider the following verses from Matthew. "Beware of false prophets, who come to you in sheep's clothing but inwardly are ravenous wolves. You will recognize them by their fruits. Are grapes gathered from thornbushes, or figs from thistles? So, every healthy tree bears good fruit, but the diseased tree bears bad fruit. A healthy tree cannot bear bad fruit, nor can a diseased tree bear good fruit. Every tree that does not bear good fruit is cut down and thrown into the fire. Thus you will recognize them by their fruits." Matthew 7:15-20

In Matthew 7:15-20, Jesus warns us that genuine fruit in one's life is not produced through external practices alone. Fruit begins within, and the tree produces what is already inside. You can fulfill religious duties while sowing discord and division among God's people. The true fruit is not attending church, reading the Bible, or bringing devotions; it is the overall impact of our lives. For the one sowing discord, it is the discord resulting from the sum total of their actions. For the one sowing unity, it is the unity resulting from the sum total of their actions. What is your life producing?

When Jesus examines the fruit of your life, what will He find? Will He find fruit that aligns with His kingdom, or will He find someone seeking to justify themselves through religious activities?

Marveling at God's Infinite Creativity

As I contemplate the world in all its intricate beauty, interdependencies, and complexities, it astounds me to imagine that God created it all from nothing. The sheer wisdom, understanding, knowledge, and boundless creativity required to create our world from nothing is beyond comprehension. It surpasses our human understanding.

When we engage in acts of creativity, we draw upon existing raw materials coupled with our experiences and knowledge. Inspired by the world around us, we craft something new. Yet, our creative endeavors pale in comparison to what God accomplished. He commenced with nothing and, within seven days, brought forth the entirety of creation. This feat is truly awe-inspiring.

Reflecting on the infinite creativity of God fills me with wonder and gratitude. It reminds me of the vastness of His power and the depths of His imagination. Every intricate detail, every harmonious interconnection, and every breathtaking marvel in our world is a testament to His unmatched creativity.

May we continue to marvel at the grandeur of God's handiwork, finding inspiration in His boundless creativity. As we engage in our creative endeavors, let us remember that we are but vessels through which His divine creativity flows, reflecting the brilliance of our Creator.

Today's Scripture

It is he who made the earth by his power, who established the world by his wisdom, and by his understanding stretched out the heavens. Jeremiah 10:12

Embracing Humility for Lasting Transformation

As I reflected last night on the challenges marriages face, I realized that, like any growing entity, marriages require nurturing and focused attention to thrive. Thinking about my marriage with Mandi, I recalled how, in our early years, I chose to listen to "Focus on the Family" instead of music during my commutes to work. This decision exposed me to invaluable insights that helped me grow as a young husband and benefited our relationship as a couple. This thought made me wonder why more individuals don't take advantage of such opportunities to grow their relationships.

I believe there are two primary reasons why many people fail to educate themselves in this regard. The first is a lack of humbleness, and the second is an unwillingness to sacrifice. In this brief reflection, I will focus on the importance of humility.

When pride consumes us, we mistakenly believe that we have all the answers and that others are to blame for our troubles. We deflect responsibility and remain oblivious to our ignorance. This pride leads us to remain trapped in our current circumstances.

However, when we humbly acknowledge that we are just as much a part of the problem as anyone else, we free ourselves to pursue solutions. Humility opens the door to improving our situation. It compels us to educate ourselves because we recognize the vast extent of what we don't know.

Today, I encourage you to release your pride and embrace humility, allowing God to lead you to a better place. Realize you don't have all the answers and seek God-given wisdom in your situation.

Today's Scripture

One's pride will bring him low, but he who is lowly in spirit will obtain honor. Proverbs 29:23

Choosing Obedience over Busyness

In our fast-paced world, we often engage in activities for the sake of busyness rather than purpose. This can distract us from spending time with God and obeying His will. We must discern which activities align with God's calling and prioritize them over those that hinder our relationship with Him.

Church activities, while important, should not automatically consume our time. We need to seek God's guidance to determine if they align with His will for us. Neglecting our spouse or family for the sake of busyness is not of God. We must consider our responsibilities and prioritize our relationships accordingly.

To prioritize obedience, we must create space to hear God's voice. By setting aside intentional time for prayer, reflection, and studying His Word, we gain clarity on the activities He has called us to do.

When we are certain of God's call to a specific activity, we must obey while ensuring we fulfill our responsibilities. This obedience may involve making sacrifices, setting boundaries, or reevaluating commitments.

Remember, God desires an intimate relationship with us. By walking with Him daily, we can ensure we are being obedient to Him and not just filling our lives with activities that distract us from God's true calling.

Today's Scripture

However, let each one of you love his wife as himself, and let the wife see that she respects her husband. Ephesians 5:33

Fathers, do not provoke your children to anger, but bring them up in the discipline and instruction of the Lord. Ephesians 6:4

Surrendering to God's Will: True Sacrifice and Worship

Throughout the Old Testament, Israel's repeated sin of worshiping other gods was a significant barrier between them and God. This transgression ultimately led to the downfall of Jerusalem. Today, modern idols have taken the form of sports, work, money, and even church or ministry. We sacrifice our devotion to the one true God when we worship these idols.

God alone is deserving of our worship and sacrifice. But what does it truly mean to offer ourselves as a sacrifice to Him? When Jesus urges us to deny ourselves, take up our cross, and follow Him, He calls us to surrender our will and embrace obedience to God's plan. Jesus demonstrated this surrender in the Garden of Gethsemane when He prayed, "not my will, but yours be done."

Truly worshiping God involves aligning our hearts, minds, and actions with His perfect purpose. It requires sacrificing our self-centered desires and choosing obedience to His will. This surrender may involve letting go of our plans, dreams, and ambitions to pursue the path God ordained.

As we offer ourselves as living sacrifices to God, remember that true worship is surrendering our will to His. May we echo the words of Jesus, "not my will, but yours be done."

Today's Scripture

Then Jesus told his disciples, If anyone would come after me, let him deny himself and take up his cross and follow me. Matthew 16:24

The Pitfalls of Coveting: Finding Contentment in God's Blessings

Coveting refers to the desire for something that belongs to someone else. This longing can encompass various aspects of life, such as material possessions, property, or even relationships. In 1 John 2:16, the "desires of the eyes" alludes to this yearning. While we often associate it with sexual desires, it extends to any desire for something others possess. It can also manifest as discontentment with the blessings God has bestowed upon us.

The lure of the "lust of the eyes" entices us with the false promise that acquiring a particular thing or person will bring us lasting happiness. However, this pursuit is an unending cycle, as our desires quickly shift to new objects of longing once we obtain what we initially craved. It is a deceptive trap orchestrated by Satan, who tells us that fulfillment is obtained through possessions or relationships.

Instead, let us embrace a mindset of contentment with the blessings God has entrusted to us and by being faithful stewards of what He has provided. If it aligns with God's will and purpose, He may choose to bless us with more. However, our contentment should not be contingent upon accumulating more but on finding joy and satisfaction in God's presence and provision.

Living in contentment frees us from the never-ending pursuit of external desires. It allows us to focus on cultivating a deeper relationship with God and seeking His guidance in aligning our desires with His plan for our lives. As we find contentment in Him, we discover fulfillment that surpasses the temporary gratification offered by worldly possessions.

Today's Scripture

For all that is in the world—the desires of the flesh and the desires of the eyes and pride in possessions—is not from the Father but is from the world. 1 John 2:16

Trusting God's Guidance in Every Decision

Last night, as I struggled to sleep, I was dealing with anxiety. It was a minor episode, perhaps an anxiety attack, triggered by the house we plan to visit today. We are seeking a new home, and this option is slightly above our initial budget. Despite seemingly meeting all our requirements based on the pictures we've seen, doubts crept in, causing restlessness.

Yesterday, I diligently evaluated the property from every angle, striving to make an informed decision. However, amid the anxious thoughts that plagued me at bedtime, I realized that I had forgotten a crucial aspect of our walk with the Lord: wholeheartedly trusting Him to guide us, even in deciding to purchase this property.

Working diligently and trusting wholeheartedly go hand in hand; they cannot be separated. When God places certain actions on our hearts, it is essential to follow through with them. Yet, trusting Him completely to oversee the situation and provide His guidance is equally vital.

While Mandi and I had sought His guidance, I had not fully trusted Him to lead us and safeguard us from making a poor decision. Proverbs 3:5-6 assures us that if we acknowledge God in all our ways, He will make our paths straight. This wisdom reminds us to take our decisions to Him, seek His guidance, and trust Him to provide it.

I encourage you to consider what you may need to bring before Him. Is there a decision, a dilemma, or a situation burdening your heart? Take the time to come before God, pour out your concerns, seek His wisdom, and relinquish control to His capable hands.

Today's Scripture

In all your ways acknowledge him, and he will make straight your paths. Proverbs 3:6

Expressing Love for God

Finding the perfect gift for someone who seemingly has everything can be challenging. Similarly, when it comes to showing our love to God, we may wonder what gift we can bring. However, God graciously reveals to us how we can express our love for Him.

1. First and foremost, we demonstrate our love for God by obeying Him. This involves seeking to understand His word as written in the Bible and actively living by its teachings. As we align our actions with His commandments, we honor Him and show our devotion. Additionally, we remain attentive to the specific guidance He imparts to us as we walk with Him daily. By obeying Him, we express our love for Him.

2. Furthermore, we love God by seeking Him earnestly. Our desire to be close to Him, to know Him intimately, and to deepen our relationship with Him reflects our love. This involves setting aside time for prayer, reading His word, and cultivating a heart that longs for His presence. As we continually seek Him wholeheartedly, we demonstrate our love for who He is.

3. Lastly, we express love for God through praise, worship, and thanksgiving. Recognizing His character, acknowledging His faithfulness, and expressing gratitude for all He has done in our lives are powerful acts of love.

In our pursuit to love God, may we continually seek to understand His word, obey His commands, and be receptive to His guidance. May we cultivate a heart that longs for His presence, desiring to know Him more each day. And may our lives resound with praise, worship, and thanksgiving, honoring Him for who He is and what He has done. In this way, we bring a precious gift to our heavenly Father—the gift of our love.

Today's Scripture

If you love me, you will keep my commandments. John 14:15

As a deer pants for flowing streams, so pants my soul for you, O God. My soul thirsts for God, for the living God. When shall I come and appear before God? Psalm 42:1-2

Let everything that has breath praise the Lord! Praise the Lord! Psalm 150:6

Embracing Humility Rather than Rivalry and Conceit

In our pursuit of personal gain and self-centered desires, we often find ourselves on a path that leads to sin. The Bible warns us against self-seeking behaviors and instead encourages us to embrace humility and consider others as more significant than ourselves. (Philippians 2:3)

When we operate from a competitive mindset, constantly comparing ourselves to others and striving to outdo them, we lose sight of the true essence of love and compassion. This mindset fosters an environment of unhealthy competition and selfish ambition, where our focus is solely on advancing our own interests at the expense of others. In this state, sin finds fertile ground to take root and flourish.

Likewise, when we are driven by conceit, consumed by our own self-importance and inflated ego, we become blind to the needs, feelings, and value of those around us. Our actions become self-centered, disregarding the impact they may have on others.

However, the remedy to this self-seeking nature lies in embracing humility. Humility enables us to recognize every individual's inherent worth and significance, treating them with respect and kindness. It is an attitude that enables us to set aside our own desires and interests and instead consider the needs of others.

In a world that often encourages self-promotion and individualism, let us heed the wisdom found in Philippians 2:3. Let us resist the temptation to pursue our interests at the expense of others. Instead, may we embrace humility, counting others as more significant than ourselves. In doing so, we create an atmosphere of love, unity, and genuine care for one another, reflecting the heart of Christ and cultivating a life pleasing to God.

Today's Scripture

Do nothing from rivalry or conceit, but in humility count others more significant than yourselves. Philippians 2:3

In What Have You Placed Your Trust?

One area where I constantly evaluate my mindset is in the realm of trust. It's important to consider what or whom I rely on for my livelihood. When fear creeps in, I often catch myself entertaining thoughts like, "I have a secure job that meets our needs," or "I have enough savings to handle any emergencies," or even "I take good care of my health, so I should be fine." However, these thoughts reveal a temptation to place my trust in something other than God to provide for and sustain me.

To truly experience God's provision and care, I must ensure that my trust is solely in Him. No job, no amount of savings, and no level of personal health can guarantee lasting security. When we trust in God, we find peace and assurance, knowing He is our ultimate provider and sustainer.

So, let us constantly examine our trust and ensure it rests solely on God. Remember that He is the only one who can truly care for us and meet our needs. He alone is faithful, dependable, and capable of providing for us in every circumstance.

Today's Scripture

For the righteous will never be moved; he will be remembered forever. He is not afraid of bad news; his heart is firm, trusting in the Lord. Psalm 112:7-8

God's Unfailing Dependability

It never ceases to amaze me how swiftly money can vanish into thin air. Even as I type these words, we find ourselves in an insurance situation that looms with uncertainty, threatening to upend our stability and leave us without a home or financial security.

Additionally, my work situation occasionally casts shadows of doubt, raising concerns about potential job loss. It's unbelievable how circumstances that once appeared rock-solid can crumble in the blink of an eye. This realization reminds us that our trust must be in God alone. He is the only one who can provide for our every need. When we wholeheartedly embrace this eternal truth and put it into practice, a peace that surpasses all understanding guards our hearts and minds.

Today's Scripture

Whoever trusts in his riches will fall, but the righteous will flourish like a green leaf. Proverbs 11:28

Breaking Free from the Victim Mindset

The victim mindset is a common pattern of thinking that permeates society. We can often find it creeping into our own minds. It is a mentality where we attribute the state of our lives solely to external factors, relinquishing our personal responsibility. I didn't have enough opportunities. I was born at the wrong time. The economy is bad, so I can't do any better financially. My marriage will never be any better because I married the wrong person. However, we must recognize the detrimental effects of this mindset and the importance of taking ownership of our situation.

Instead of blaming others or external circumstances, we must focus on our actions and personal responsibility. Rather than seeing ourselves as helpless victims, we can choose to own the situation and take action to change it.

Here are some examples of taking ownership of our situation. I will ask for more opportunities or create my own. I will create something great regardless of the time I'm born. I will educate myself and create opportunities even in a bad economy. What can I do differently to improve my marriage? My happiness doesn't depend on another person.

So, when we find ourselves slipping into the victim mindset, let us pause and remind ourselves that we serve a big God. He can bring us through this circumstance and grow our character in the process. By taking ownership of our thoughts, actions, and decisions, we can break free from the limitations of victimhood and embrace a mindset of ownership, resilience, and personal responsibility.

Today's Scripture

Do not be conformed to this world, but be transformed by the renewal of your mind, that by testing you may discern what is the will of God, what is good and acceptable and perfect. Romans 12:2

The Destructive Nature of Pride

Pride is a powerful force that can lead us down a destructive path. It hinders us from seeking forgiveness and prevents us from extending forgiveness to others. It isolates us from the support and friendship we need in difficult times. Pride closes our eyes to the wisdom and guidance of others, causing us to disregard instruction and rebuke. It deceives us into thinking we can sin without consequences and leads us to take on tasks or responsibilities we are not ready for, often resulting in negative outcomes. Worst of all, pride can influence us to lead others astray.

In contrast, humility is the antidote to pride. Humility enables us to ask for forgiveness when we have wronged others. It allows us to extend forgiveness, recognizing the great forgiveness we have received ourselves.

Humility prompts us to seek help and support from those around us instead of isolating ourselves. It opens our hearts and minds to listen to wise counsel and learn from others. Above all, humility is essential in our relationship with God, as it acknowledges our dependence on Him and enables us to walk in His ways.

Recognizing the destructive nature of pride, we should cultivate a spirit of humility. Let us strive to be humble in our interactions with others, acknowledging our shortcomings and embracing the opportunity for growth and transformation. By embracing humility, we can experience the freedom that comes from genuine repentance, reconciliation, and a deeper connection with God and those around us.

Today's Scripture

When pride comes, then comes disgrace, but with the humble is wisdom. Proverbs 11:2

Confidence in God

Take a moment to read Today's Scripture, then come back here.

In 1 John 5, we discover the confidence that comes from praying according to God's will. But how do we discern if our requests align with His will?

1. Firstly, we should ensure that our prayers are not contrary to the Word of God. Anything that contradicts the teachings of the Bible is not in line with His will. God will never lead us to pray for something that goes against His revealed truth.

2. Secondly, developing a close relationship with God is crucial. Spending time with Him, seeking His presence, and listening for His voice in quiet moments will help us discern His will. As we grow our relationship with Him, His desires become clearer.

3. Thirdly, seeking godly counsel can provide valuable insights. Consulting trusted and mature believers who are grounded in the Word can help us discern God's will more effectively.

These three factors—aligning our prayers with Scripture, cultivating intimacy with God, and seeking wise counsel—work together to confirm that we are indeed praying according to God's will.

However, there are instances when God may choose not to reveal His will. In such cases, we can still bring our requests to Him, praying for what we know and trusting that God has our best interests, as well as the best interests of others, in mind.

So let us approach God with confidence, knowing that as we align our prayers with His will, we have what we have requested of Him. And when His will remains a mystery, we can trust in His wisdom and rest in the assurance that He works all things for our ultimate good.

Today's Scripture

And this is the confidence that we have toward him, that if we ask anything according to his will he hears us. And if we know that he hears us in whatever we ask, we know that we have the requests that we have asked of him. 1 John 5:14-15

Counting the Cost for Jesus

Throughout history, countless followers of Jesus have faced persecution and even death for their unwavering commitment to Him. Today, believers still endure imprisonment, violence, and even loss of life for their faith in some parts of the world. Although the current situation in the United States may not involve such extreme measures, there is a growing intolerance towards biblical truths that may lead to increased challenges and potential persecution in the future.

In light of this, we must examine our hearts and consider what we are willing to give up or lose for the sake of Jesus and His Word. Are we prepared to stand firm in our faith even in the face of opposition? Are there attachments in this world that could cause us to renounce Jesus or compromise our beliefs?

Certain biblical truths may clash with societal norms or workplace policies, potentially resulting in adverse consequences. The question then becomes, are we willing to bear the cost? Are we willing to risk our employment or face severe penalties for standing by those truths?

As followers of Jesus, our allegiance is to Him above all else. It requires a willingness to surrender worldly comforts, security, and even our own lives if called upon. It demands unwavering faith, trust, and obedience. While our circumstances may vary, the question remains: Will we choose to wholeheartedly follow Jesus, even amid persecution and loss?

Let us seek the strength and courage to remain steadfast, knowing God's grace is sufficient for us. May we find encouragement in the examples of those who have gone before us, and may we rely on the power of the Holy Spirit to help us stand firm in the face of any challenges that may come our way.

Today's Scripture

Blessed is the man who remains steadfast under trial, for when he has stood the test he will receive the crown of life, which God has promised to those who love him. James 1:12

Freedom from Condemnation in Christ

One of the most powerful weapons in Satan's arsenal is the condemnation he unleashes upon us when we make mistakes. This condemnation makes us feel unworthy to stand in God's presence or engage in His work, which is precisely what Satan wants. He wants us to stop doing God's work and destroy our relationship with God.

Amidst this condemnation, we must hold onto the truth that no sacrifice, apart from the blood of Jesus Christ, can truly wipe away our transgressions. When we turn back to God, genuinely repenting, He immediately forgives us and casts our sins into the sea of His forgetfulness. From that point on, He no longer holds our sins against us. We become worthy to enter God's presence because of the sacrificial blood of Jesus Christ and the price He paid on our behalf.

Now, let us reject condemnation, roll up our sleeves and get back to the work God has called us to do.

Today's Scripture

There is therefore now no condemnation for those who are in Christ Jesus. For the law of the life-giving Spirit in Christ Jesus has set you free from the law of sin and death. Romans 8:1-2

Embracing God's Ongoing Transformation

On this side of heaven, we are continually being shaped by God's hand. His work within us is a constant process, unveiling areas needing His cleansing touch. Our prayer needs to be for God to search and reveal any hidden sins. However, we must resist the temptation to dwell in fear and condemnation over unknown sins.

If the Holy Spirit has NOT brought sins to your attention, rest assured that He will make you aware of them in His perfect timing. We need not fret over what He has not revealed to us.

Instead, our focus should be on deepening our relationship with God. As we draw near Him, He will continue purifying and transforming us. Let us embrace the ongoing work of God within us, trusting His wisdom and timing to change us into who He wants us to be.

Today's Scripture

Examine me, O God, and probe my thoughts. Test me, and know my concerns. See if there is any idolatrous way in me, and lead me in the everlasting way. Psalm 139:23-24

The Impact of Relationships

The individuals we spend the most time with significantly influence our lives. If we don't want to be like the people around us, we must reconsider the company we keep. No matter how strong-willed we may be, the influence of others remains a fundamental law of human relationships, much like the force of gravity in nature.

God, in His wisdom, understands this principle of relationships. In the Old Testament, He cautioned the Israelites against intermarrying with pagans, fully aware it would lead His people into sin. This idea of influence underscores the significance of being part of a community of believers. Being around individuals who actively seek God influences our own walk with Him. It helps us remain steadfast, remain on course, and nurture our trust in God. Church, therefore, plays a pivotal role in fostering spiritual growth and accountability.

Let us be mindful of the relationships we cultivate, recognizing their potential to shape our character and faith. Our relationships will determine the person we become a year from now. May we actively seek companions who share our passion for seeking God as we strive to walk in His ways.

Today's Scripture

Do not be deceived: Bad company ruins good morals. 1 Corinthians 15:33

Embracing the Call to Surrender

In this devotional, I believe it's important to begin with the scripture passage to provide context. This concept is often overlooked in our churches yet holds profound significance in our spiritual lives.

Then Jesus told his disciples, If anyone would come after me, let him deny himself and take up his cross and follow me. For whoever would save his life will lose it, but whoever loses his life for my sake will find it. For what will it profit a man if he gains the whole world and forfeits his soul? Or what shall a man give in return for his soul? Matthew 16:24-26

We are called to hold loosely to earthly possessions and be willing to surrender everything to Him. God knows the destructiveness of worldly possessions. If we cling too tightly to them, they can gradually consume us and lead us astray. I'm not saying that having stuff is bad, but the stuff cannot get in the way of our obedience to God.

By surrendering our lives to God and embracing His calling, we open ourselves to the fullness of His blessings. He longs to fill our lives with joy, peace, love, and hope that surpasses what the world can offer. Is there anything you would not let go of in your life to follow God? I encourage you to surrender it to Him today.

Trusting God's Unfailing Refuge

Amidst the uncertainties of our country's economy and the challenges in my life, seeking refuge in God holds great appeal. Oxford Languages defines refuge as "a condition of being safe or sheltered from pursuit, danger, or trouble." In these tumultuous times, finding solace and protection in God resonates deeply. Whether we face prosperity or adversity, God is our true and unwavering refuge. Trusting in anything or anyone else is futile, as friends, family, jobs, and money will ultimately fail us. Only God remains steadfast.

Embracing God's refuge brings numerous benefits, especially amid uncertainty and turmoil. When everything around us is in upheaval, the knowledge that God will protect and preserve us brings peace that surpasses human understanding. We must consider where our trust truly lies. Let us place our unwavering trust in God, the ultimate refuge, and experience the profound peace and security that only He can provide.

Today's Scripture

I cry to you, O Lord; I say, You are my refuge, my portion in the land of the living. Psalm 142:5

Active Waiting: Trusting and Seeking God's Answer

Waiting on the Lord is an active and purposeful endeavor. When we find ourselves waiting on God, it usually means we are anticipating His response to our prayers. It could be a crucial decision we need guidance on or a situation requiring His intervention. Whatever it is, we pray earnestly and enter a season of waiting.

So, how should we navigate this waiting period? First and foremost, we persevere in prayer, consistently bringing our needs before God. Jesus emphasized the importance of persistence in prayer through a parable, encouraging us to remain steadfast.

Additionally, we place our complete trust in God alone. We resist the temptation to rely on anyone or anything else to answer our prayers. Our faith is solely anchored in God's faithfulness.

While waiting, we continue to nurture our relationship with God, investing time to deepen our connection with Him. This time of waiting serves as an opportunity for God to draw us nearer to Him. We diligently seek His presence, devoting ourselves to daily communion with Him.

It is essential to bring our doubts and uncertainties before God. We can ask Him to help us overcome any disbelief we may experience. Seeking God when we have doubt is an act of faith in His ability to provide answers.

As we actively wait on the Lord, we trust, seek, and persist in prayer, allowing our faith to grow and our relationship with Him to flourish.

Today's Scripture

The Lord is good to those who wait for him, to the soul who seeks him. Lamentations 3:25

Our Identity in Christ

Who are we? It's a question that often lingers in our minds.

We tend to seek our identity in job titles, achievements, and material possessions. We may even associate our identity with the experiences we've had or the activities we enjoy. But what happens when our job is lost or we can no longer perform it? What if our possessions are stripped away? And how would we respond if we could not engage in what we enjoy? If we desire a firm foundation that lasts a lifetime, we must discover our true identity in Christ.

According to 2 Corinthians 5:17, "Therefore, if anyone is in Christ, he is a new creation. The old has passed away; behold, the new has come." When we invite Christ into our lives, we undergo a transformation. Our former selves, marked by sin and brokenness, are washed away, and we are made new in Him.

Furthermore, Ephesians 2:10 tells us, "For we are his workmanship, created in Christ Jesus for good works, which God prepared beforehand, that we should walk in them." We are God's masterpiece, intricately crafted with purpose. Our calling is to do the good works He has prepared for us.

Our identity does not reside in our job, achievements, experiences, pleasures, or possessions. Our true identity is discovered in Christ. As we live out our purpose in Him, we will encounter the fullness of life He offers. Jesus referred to it as an abundant life in John 10:10.

Today's Scripture

For we are his workmanship, created in Christ Jesus for good works, which God prepared beforehand, that we should walk in them. Ephesians 2:10

Fear as a Call to Return to God

Fear can serve as a powerful indicator in our lives, especially when it stems from living in sin. The Holy Spirit convicts us of our wrongdoing, but at times, we choose to ignore the conviction or find ways to rationalize our actions, believing they are acceptable.

This resistance to acknowledging our sins leads to an underlying fear of facing God's judgment. Our days become consumed by anxiety, anticipating God's discipline or punishment. If fear dominates your life, it may be time to examine whether sin is at its root. Take a moment to seek God's guidance, listening attentively in the quietness of your heart. Pay careful attention to what God brings to mind. Are you attempting to justify something that God declares as wrong?

Release your grip on those justifications and allow God to bring peace to your fears. He is ready to extend His forgiveness if you sincerely seek it. Surrender to Him, confess your sins, and experience the assurance that comes from being reconciled with your Heavenly Father. Through God's forgiveness, you will find strength and courage.

Today's Scripture

If we confess our sins, he is faithful and just to forgive us our sins and to cleanse us from all unrighteousness. 1 John 1:9

The Transformative Power of Forgiveness

Forgiveness holds immense power. It can mend shattered relationships, mend wounded hearts, and renew our hope. However, it can also be one of our most challenging tasks. We often cling to grudges and harbor bitterness, allowing them to consume us, inflicting pain, and creating a divide between us and God.

Forgiveness is not merely a kind gesture; it is a divine command. Jesus emphasized, "For if you forgive others their trespasses, your heavenly Father will also forgive you, but if you do not forgive others their trespasses, neither will your Father forgive your trespasses." (Matthew 6:14-15).

When we choose to forgive, we are not only obeying God but we are also unburdening ourselves from anger and resentment. We place our trust in God, believing He will handle the situation in His own perfect way and timing.

Forgiveness is not always easy, and it does not mean forgetting what transpired or condoning the actions of others. Instead, it means releasing the pain and loving the person, even if they never apologize or make amends.

In Colossians 3:13, it instructs us to "bearing with one another and, if one has a complaint against another, forgiving each other; as the Lord has forgiven you, so you also must forgive." As we learn to extend forgiveness to others, we experience the transformative power of God's forgiveness in our own lives. We are freed from the chains of unforgiveness and can walk in the serenity and joy that forgiveness brings.

Is there someone in your life whom you need to forgive? Though challenging, remember the remarkable power of forgiveness. Choose to obey God's command, release the burden of bitterness, and place your trust in Him. By doing so, you will encounter the freedom that comes from extending forgiveness to others.

Today's Scripture

For if you forgive others their trespasses, your heavenly Father will also forgive you, but if you do not forgive others their trespasses, neither will your Father forgive your trespasses. Matthew 6:14-15

A Triad of Growth

In the final three devotions, we will explore three distinct aspects of how God nurtures our faith, forming a powerful triad of growth. Each of these components is indispensable, and omitting any of them can hinder the development of our faith. Here's a diagram summarizing this triad of growth to provide a glimpse of what lies ahead.

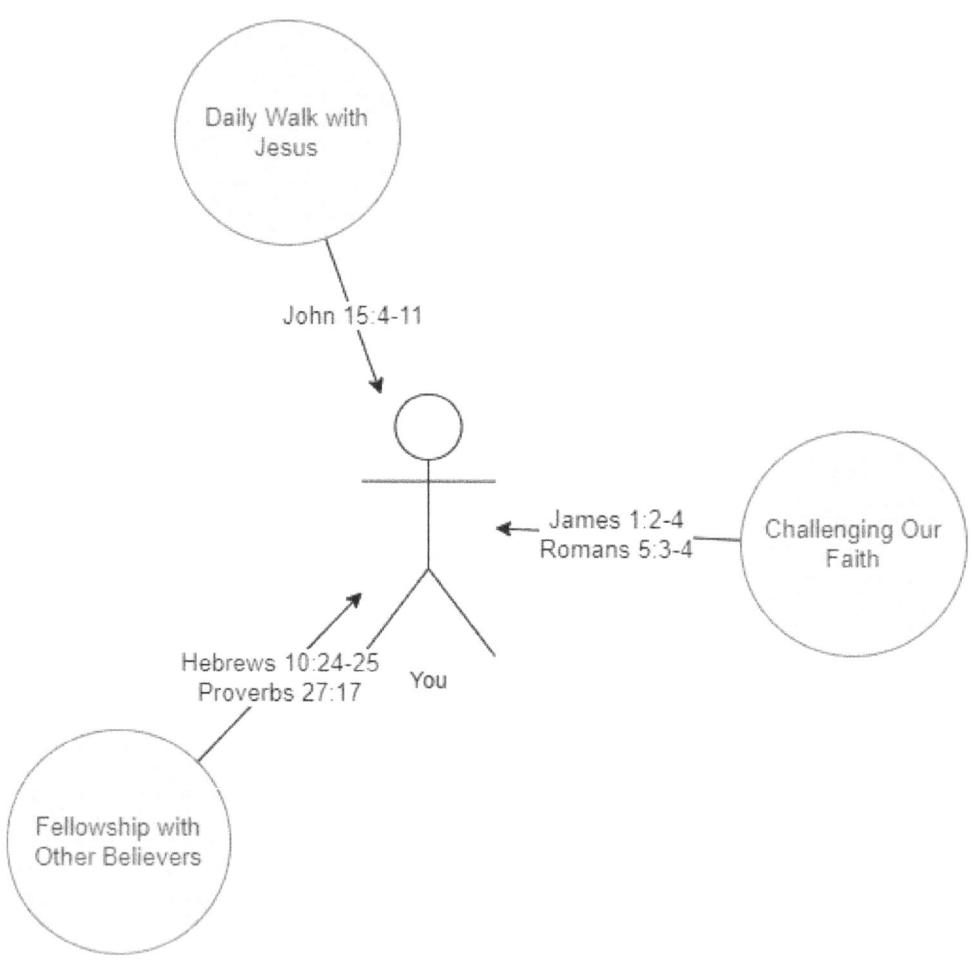

Challenging Our Faith

Mandi and I were in the market for a stock trailer some time ago. Until then, we had been borrowing trailers to transport our animals to the butcher. However, we realized we needed a dependable trailer of our own to ensure a smooth and worry-free process. After finding one that suited our needs, we made the purchase. We were confident in its potential, although it required some repairs, particularly the floor.

I took the trailer to my brother, Michael, who is skilled in fixing such things. While working on it, he addressed the floor and brought to my attention several other issues that needed attention. My fixer-upper was more of a project than I had initially thought.

One significant problem was the support beam running along the length of the trailer. These beams were crucial for providing the main support for the floor. As Michael welded additional bracing between them, he discovered the beams were thin in some areas.

With the plan to transport three large steers to the butcher in a week, we knew the newly braced floor would face a real test. These hefty steers, weighing around 1500 pounds each, were bound to put the floor's strength to the ultimate challenge.

The day arrived for us to load the steers into the trailer and put it to the test. As they moved around, the floor flexed under their weight. In addition, they would often turn in circles, further assessing the floor's durability. Occasionally, they would find a spot to stand still for a few minutes before circling again. I inspected the thinned support beams with my flashlight throughout this rigorous test. Surprisingly, despite the strain on the floor, everything appeared to be in order.

We embarked on the hour-long journey to the butcher, stopping to inspect the beams several times. To my relief, they held up just fine. The additional bracing strengthened the wooden floorboards and helped distribute the weight evenly, compensating for the thin areas in the beams.

This testing of the trailer floor parallels the testing our faith undergoes. It is not a pass-or-fail test but an opportunity to strengthen what is already present. Just as bodybuilders challenge their muscles to enhance strength, our faith grows when challenged. While our faith may bend and flex under the weight of challenges, when we trust God, He ensures we do not break under the heavy load. In fact, Jesus invites us in Matthew 11:28, saying, " Come to me, all who labor and are heavy laden, and I will give you rest." Amidst the trials of our faith, we can turn to Him and find rest.

Why does God desire to cultivate and develop our faith? There are several reasons behind His purpose. Firstly, He seeks to draw us closer to Himself, fostering a deeper connection with us. Additionally, God intends to equip us with spiritual strength for the tasks He has in store. Just as one cannot instantly transition from lifting 10 pounds to lifting 150 pounds in the gym, our faith requires gradual growth and strengthening over time.

Moreover, God desires to positively impact the lives of those around us. When our faith becomes robust and resilient, like a rising tide lifting all ships, it influences and inspires those who observe it. As they witness the strength of our faith, their own faith is encouraged and fortified. This leads us to the second aspect of our triad of growth.

Today's Scripture

Count it all joy, my brothers, when you meet trials of various kinds, for you know that the testing of your faith produces steadfastness. And let steadfastness have its full effect, that you may be perfect and complete, lacking in nothing.   James 1:2-4

More than that, we rejoice in our sufferings, knowing that suffering produces endurance, and endurance produces character, and character produces hope, Romans 5:3-4

Walking with Other Christians

There's a common saying in personal growth circles that states you become the average of the five people you spend the most time with. While I can't confirm its exact accuracy, one thing is certain: we significantly influence one another. The more we interact with someone, the greater their impact on our lives. Hence, it becomes crucial to choose our friends wisely.

This thought brings us to the second way our faith grows. When we surround ourselves with people with strong faith, we can observe their actions, reactions, and mindset. We begin to adopt their way of thinking and behaving. We learn from their faith and even from their failures. The Holy Spirit uses these lessons to refine and sharpen our faith. They become a source of encouragement when we need it; likewise, we offer support when they need it.

It's important to note that the scriptures don't advocate for casting someone aside due to their mistakes or engaging in gossip about their shortcomings. Instead, they emphasize the power of encouragement and stirring one another towards love and good works.

Do you regularly gather with a community of Christians where you mutually shape and uplift one another with love and encouragement?

Speaking of people influencing us, who is better to influence us than Jesus Christ Himself? That is precisely what tomorrow's devotion will explore.

Today's Scripture

And let us consider how to stir up one another to love and good works, not neglecting to meet together, as is the habit of some, but encouraging one another, and all the more as you see the Day drawing near. Hebrews 10:24-25

Iron sharpens iron, and one man sharpens another. Proverbs 27:17

Daily Walk with Jesus

Our daily walk with Jesus should resemble a branch connected to a tree. Just as a branch never decides it doesn't need the tree and disconnects to do its own thing, we must stay connected to Jesus for daily nourishment and strength. This walk with Jesus provides us with friendship and encouragement. It also serves as a compass to guide us and correct our course when we stray down the wrong path.

As the previous day's devotion discussed, we are strongly influenced by those we spend time with. Who better to be influenced by than Jesus himself? We want our mindset, beliefs, and actions to be like His. So let's spend a lot of time with Him.

What's more, this relationship provides us with joy. I want to encourage you to pause and read Today's Scripture. Take note of the last sentence, where we see that joy stems from our relationship with Jesus.

Furthermore, relationships are never stagnant; they are either growing or shrinking. To foster a thriving relationship with Jesus, we must invest time in His presence and communicate with Him regularly. Are you dedicating daily time to be with Jesus, immersing yourself in His Word and conversing with Him? If you do, your faith will deepen as you experience friendship, strength, joy, mercy, forgiveness, truth, and so much more.

Today's Scripture

Abide in me, and I in you. As the branch cannot bear fruit by itself, unless it abides in the vine, neither can you, unless you abide in me. I am the vine; you are the branches. Whoever abides in me and I in him, he it is that bears much fruit, for apart from me you can do nothing. If anyone does not abide in me he is thrown away like a branch and withers; and the branches are gathered, thrown into the fire, and burned. If you abide in me, and my words abide in you, ask whatever you wish, and it will be done for you. By this my Father is glorified, that you bear much fruit and so prove to be my disciples. As the Father has loved me, so have I loved you. Abide in my love. If you keep my commandments, you will abide in my love, just as I have kept my Father's commandments and abide in his love. These things I have spoken to you, that my joy may be in you, and that your joy may be full. John 15:4-11

Where Do We Go From Here?

I hope your relationship deepened as you grew in understanding who God is, His will, and the relationship He wants to have with you. But what comes next? I encourage you to continue investing in your quiet time with God. Just as any relationship requires nurturing, so does our relationship with Him. Set aside dedicated time to spend with God, allowing Him to communicate with you through His Word and pouring out your heart to Him in prayer.

You don't necessarily need a daily devotion to sustain your quiet time. Simply reading a chapter a day from the Bible can be a great way to continue growing. You might consider starting with the book of Proverbs. As you read, allow the Holy Spirit to highlight and speak to you through the verses that stand out.

However, I want to caution you against allowing your time with God to become routine. Approach your moments with Him as if you are spending time with the most important person in your life – because truly, no one is more significant than your Creator, Father, and Friend.

Cultivate a genuine desire to know Him more deeply, to draw closer to His heart, and to apply His Word in your daily life. Remember, His love for you surpasses anything you can imagine. Seek to strengthen your faith, finding joy, strength, and unwavering hope that anchors your soul through every season. Walk confidently, knowing that God is faithfully walking beside you every step of the way.

Today's Scripture

Now may the God of peace who brought again from the dead our Lord Jesus, the great shepherd of the sheep, by the blood of the eternal covenant, equip you with everything good that you may do his will, working in us that which is pleasing in his sight, through Jesus Christ, to whom be glory forever and ever. Amen. Hebrews 13:20-21

Author Bio

Eric is a devoted husband, father, and passionate follower of Jesus Christ. With a deep-rooted desire to help people grow in their relationship with Christ, Eric has embarked on a mission to share the wisdom and understanding he has gained from God's Word. Whether through his writing or speaking engagements, he wholeheartedly dedicates himself to uplifting and inspiring others on their journey with Jesus.

Eric's experiences as a husband and father have provided him with valuable insights into the challenges and joys of life. Through his personal growth and struggles, he has discovered the transformative power of a vibrant relationship with Jesus, and he is passionate about guiding others in cultivating meaningful connections with the Savior.

When Eric stands before a group of individuals, his heart is filled with a genuine desire to impact their lives. His words resonate with hope, encouragement, and practical wisdom, helping listeners to deepen their faith in Christ.

Eric's dedication to helping others grow in Christ shines through his compassionate nature and commitment to serving those around him. Through his book, "Daily Walking with God: 90 Short Devotionals to Deepen Your Relationship with Him," he invites readers to embark on a transformative journey, embracing God's presence in their daily lives.

Made in the USA
Monee, IL
31 August 2023

41920364R10075